DELIBERATE PRACTICE IN

MOTIVATIONAL INTERVIEWING

Essentials of Deliberate Practice Series
Tony Rousmaniere and Alexandre Vaz, Series Editors

ESSENTIALS OF DELIBERATE PRACTICE SERIES

TONY ROUSMANIERE AND ALEXANDRE VAZ, SERIES EDITORS

DELIBERATE PRACTICE IN
MOTIVATIONAL INTERVIEWING

JENNIFER K. MANUEL

DENISE ERNST

ALEXANDRE VAZ

TONY ROUSMANIERE

AMERICAN PSYCHOLOGICAL ASSOCIATION

Published by
American Psychological Association
750 First Street, NE
Washington, DC 20002
https://www.apa.org

Order Department
https://www.apa.org/pubs/books
order@apa.org

In the U.K., Europe, Africa, and the Middle East, copies may be ordered from Eurospan
https://www.eurospanbookstore.com/apa
info@eurospangroup.com

Typeset in Cera Pro by Circle Graphics, Inc., Reisterstown, MD

Printer: Gasch Printing, Odenton, MD
Cover Designer: Naylor Design, Washington, DC

Library of Congress Cataloging-in-Publication Data

Names: Manuel, Jennifer K., author. | Ernst, Denise, author. | Vaz, Alexandre, author. |
    Rousmaniere, Tony, author.
Title: Deliberate practice in motivational interviewing / by Jennifer K. Manuel,
    Denise Ernst, Alexandre Vaz, and Tony Rousmaniere.
Description: Washington, DC : American Psychological Association, 2022. |
    Series: Essentials of deliberate practice | Includes bibliographical
    references and index.
Identifiers: LCCN 2021060928 (print) | LCCN 2021060929 (ebook) |
    ISBN 9781433836183 (paperback) | ISBN 9781433836190 (ebook)
Subjects: LCSH: Motivational interviewing. | Counseling psychology. |
    BISAC: PSYCHOLOGY / Education & Training | PSYCHOLOGY / Clinical Psychology
Classification: LCC BF637.I5 M356 2022 (print) | LCC BF637.I5 (ebook) |
    DDC 158.3/9--dc23/eng/20220308
LC record available at https://lccn.loc.gov/2021060928
LC ebook record available at https://lccn.loc.gov/2021060929

https://doi.org/10.1037/0000297-000

Printed in the United States of America

10 9 8 7 6 5 4 3 2

Contents

Series Preface

Tony Rousmaniere and Alexandre Vaz

We are pleased to introduce the Essentials of Deliberate Practice series of training books. We are developing this book series to address a specific need that we see in many psychology training programs. The issue can be illustrated by the training experiences of Mary, a hypothetical second-year graduate school trainee. Mary has learned a lot about mental health theory, research, and psychotherapy techniques. Mary is a dedicated student; she has read dozens of textbooks, written excellent papers about psychotherapy, and receives near-perfect scores on her course exams. However, when Mary sits with her clients at her practicum site, she often has trouble performing the therapy skills that she can write and talk about so clearly. Furthermore, Mary has noticed herself getting anxious when her clients express strong reactions, such as getting very emotional, hopeless, or skeptical about therapy. Sometimes this anxiety is strong enough to make Mary freeze at key moments, limiting her ability to help those clients.

During her weekly individual and group supervision, Mary's supervisor gives her advice informed by empirically supported therapies and common factor methods. The supervisor often supplements that advice by leading Mary through role-plays, recommending additional reading, or providing examples from her own work with clients. Mary, a dedicated supervisee who shares tapes of her sessions with her supervisor, is open about her challenges, carefully writes down her supervisor's advice, and reads the suggested readings. However, when Mary sits back down with her clients, she often finds that her new knowledge seems to have flown out of her head, and she is unable to enact her supervisor's advice. Mary finds this problem to be particularly acute with the clients who are emotionally evocative.

Mary's supervisor, who has received formal training in supervision, uses supervisory best practices, including the use of video to review supervisees' work. She would rate Mary's overall competence level as consistent with expectations for a trainee at Mary's developmental level. But even though Mary's overall progress is positive, she experiences some recurring problems in her work. This is true even though the supervisor is confident that she and Mary have identified the changes that Mary should make in her work.

The problem with which Mary and her supervisor are wrestling—the disconnect between her knowledge about psychotherapy and her ability to reliably perform psychotherapy—is the focus of this book series. We started this series because most therapists experience this disconnect, to one degree or another, whether they are beginning trainees or highly experienced clinicians. In truth, we are all Mary.

To address this problem, we are focusing this series on the use of deliberate practice, a method of training specifically designed for improving reliable performance of complex skills in challenging work environments (Rousmaniere, 2016, 2019; Rousmaniere et al., 2017). Deliberate practice entails experiential, repeated training with a particular skill until it becomes automatic. In the context of psychotherapy, this involves two trainees role-playing as a client and a therapist, switching roles every so often, under the guidance of a supervisor. The trainee playing the therapist reacts to client statements, ranging in difficulty from beginner to intermediate to advanced, with improvised responses that reflect fundamental therapeutic skills.

To create these books, we approached leading trainers and researchers of major therapy models with these simple instructions: Identify 12 essential skills for your therapy model where trainees often experience a disconnect between cognitive knowledge and performance ability—in other words, skills that trainees could write a good paper about but often have challenges performing, especially with challenging clients. We then collaborated with the authors to create deliberate practice exercises specifically designed to improve reliable performance of these skills and overall responsive treatment (Hatcher, 2015; Stiles et al., 1998; Stiles & Horvath, 2017). Finally, we rigorously tested these exercises with trainees and trainers at multiple sites around the world and refined them based on extensive feedback.

Each book in this series focuses on a specific therapy model, but readers will notice that most exercises in these books touch on common factor variables and facilitative interpersonal skills that researchers have identified as having the most impact on client outcome, such as empathy, verbal fluency, emotional expression, persuasiveness, and problem focus (e.g., Anderson et al., 2009; Norcross et al., 2019). Thus, the exercises in every book should help with a broad range of clients. Despite the specific theoretical model(s) from which therapists work, most therapists place a strong emphasis on pantheoretical elements of the therapeutic relationship, many of which have robust empirical support as correlates or mechanisms of client improvement (e.g., Norcross et al., 2019). We also recognize that therapy models have already-established training programs with rich histories, so we present deliberate practice not as a replacement but as an adaptable, transtheoretical training method that can be integrated into these existing programs to improve skill retention and help ensure basic competency.

About This Book

This book in the series is on motivational interviewing (MI), a client-centered approach for facilitating behavior change (Miller & Rollnick, 2013). MI is best suited for clients who are ambivalent about engaging in behavior change and is often used as a precursor to other formalized treatments (e.g., cognitive behavioral therapy). MI is a nuanced approach, and many trainees find that a multifaceted approach to learning is required to achieve MI competence. This multifaceted approach includes reading on the theory of MI (e.g., Miller & Rollnick, 2013), practice of MI skills, and feedback from peer or supervisor observers. The maxim "learning by doing" is appropriate in MI learning. A trainee may read about MI and be knowledgeable about the theory of it, but this knowledge may not translate to direct clinical skills. Practicing MI skills, with ongoing feedback, is needed to build and deepen a clinician's use of MI in clinical settings.

In this book, we adopt deliberate practice methods to support experiential—learn by doing—training opportunities. The described methods and stimuli can facilitate practicing a range of important MI skills. In addition, the book supports fine-tuning the "how" of intervention delivery, including in a flexible manner across diverse clinical scenarios. Importantly, this book is not intended to replace core coursework and exposure to foundational MI theory and principles of practice. Rather, it is intended to augment other common training components.

Acknowledgments

We'd like to acknowledge Rodney Goodyear for his significant contribution to starting and organizing this book series. We are grateful to Susan Reynolds, David Becker, Elizabeth Budd, and Emily Ekle at the American Psychological Association (APA) for providing expert guidance and insightful editing that has significantly improved the quality and accessibility of this book. Our deepest gratitude to Bill Miller and Steve Rollnick, cocreators of motivational interviewing (MI), for their vision and early advocacy that led to fundamental shifts in the treatment of individuals with addiction and other mental health disorders. We are especially grateful to Bill for his mentorship and commitment to training and education. We thank Terri Moyers for her incredible contributions to MI training and supervision. Finally, we are appreciative of the invaluable editorial notes and feedback from Inês Amaro, Amy DeSmidt, and Jamie Manser.

The exercises in this book underwent extensive testing at training programs around the world. We are deeply grateful to the following supervisors and trainees who tested exercises and provided invaluable feedback:

- Inês Amaro, Psinove, Lisbon, Portugal

- Myriam N. Bechtoldt, EBS Universität für Wirtschaft and Recht, Oestrich-Winkel, Germany

- Patrick Bennett, Einstein Medical Center, Philadelphia, PA, United States

- Annie Fahy, Anisse Puryear, Barbara Garcia, and Karina Roderiguez, Annie Fahy Consulting, Asheville, NC, United States

- Cristiana Fortini, Miranda Sanson, and Noémie Jeanmonod, CHUV, Lausanne, Switzerland

- Ali Hall, Ali Hall Training and Consulting, San Francisco, CA, United States

- Sky Kershner, Rev Matt Johnson, and Sheila Zickefoose, West Virginia University School of Medicine, Morgantown, WV, United States

- Ken Kraybill, C4 Innovations, Seattle, WA, United States

- Jennifer Langhinrichsen-Rohling, Grace Carter, Bridget Jules, Dana Miller, Ameante Payen, Pedram Rastegar, Alexa Sotiroff, and Tran Tran, University of North Carolina at Charlotte, Charlotte, NC, United States

- Anita McGregor, Leah Vircoe, Cooper Jackson, Aston Wisken, and Shaye Elia, University of New South Wales, Sydney, Australia

- Helen Mentha, Mentha Consulting, Melbourne, Australia

- Rosemarie Campos Sachs, Jorge Masdeu, and Rodolfo Andre Castelo, private practice, San Diego, CA, United States

- Michelle Stephen Seigel, Prevention Research Institute, Lexington, KY, United States

- Catarina Telo and Georgia Gold, South West London and St George's Mental Health NHS Trust, London, England, United Kingdom

- Lianna Trubowitz, Ferkauf Graduate School of Psychology, Bronx, NY, United States

- Alix Velasco, The Welsh Psychotherapy Institute, Newport, Wales, United Kingdom

- Kate Watson, The Advocacy Academy, Philadelphia, PA, United States

- Mingxin Wei, private practice, Baltimore, MD, United States

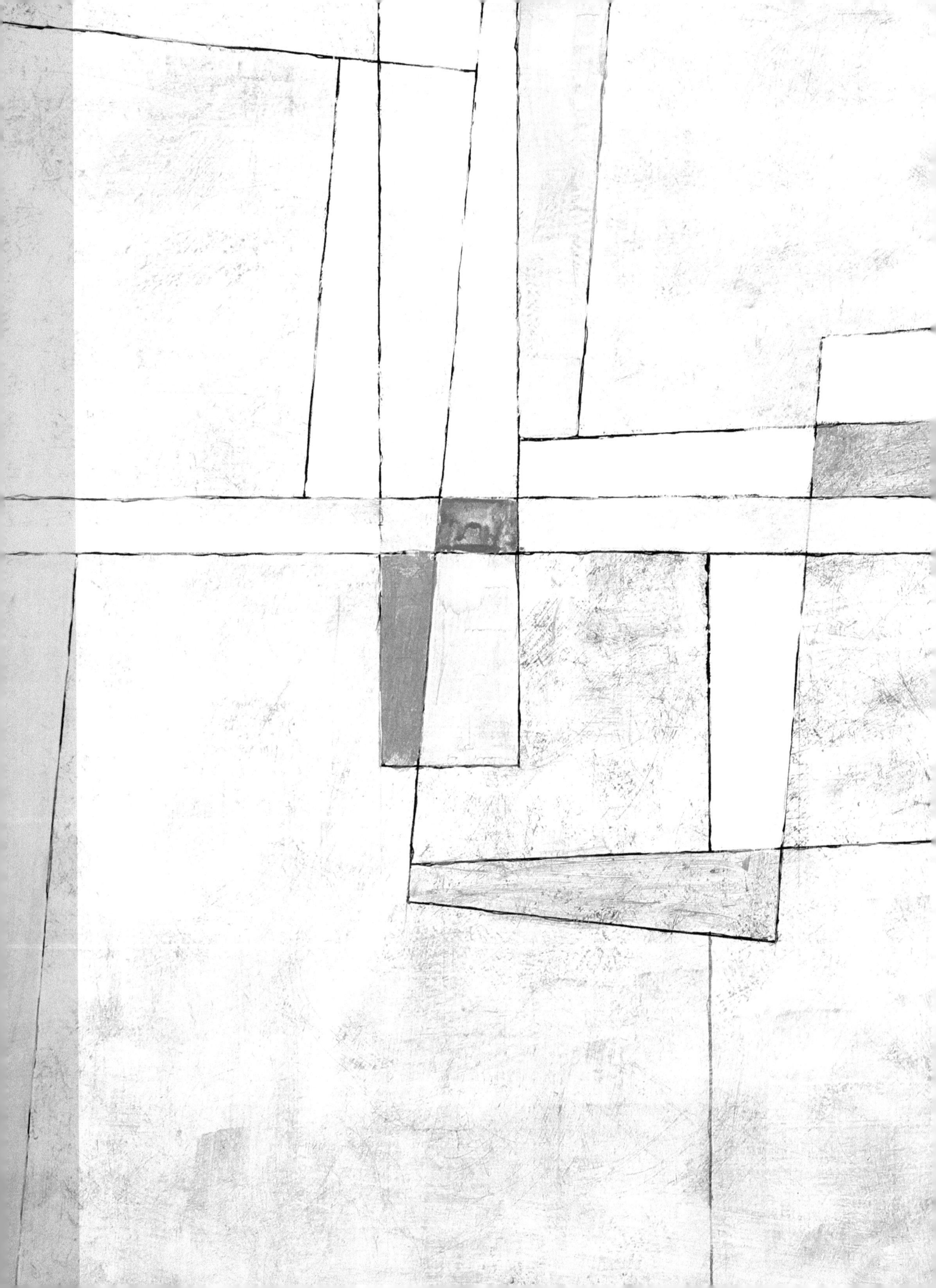

Overview and Instructions

In Part I, we provide an overview of deliberate practice, including how it can be integrated into motivational interviewing (MI) training programs and instructions for performing the deliberate practice exercises in Part II. **We encourage both trainers and trainees to read both Chapters 1 and 2 before performing the deliberate practice exercises for the first time.**

Chapter 1 provides a foundation for the rest of the book by introducing important concepts related to deliberate practice and its role in training more broadly and MI training more specifically. We review key MI skills—reflective listening, affirmations, autonomy support statements, and the role of client language in MI all covered in the deliberate practice exercises in Part II. We also individually review the 12 skills from these exercises.

Chapter 2 lays out the basic, most essential instructions for performing the MI practice exercises in Part II. They are designed to be quick and simple and provide you with just enough information to get started without being overwhelmed by too much information. Chapter 3 in Part III provides more in-depth guidance, which we encourage you to read once you are comfortable with the basic instructions in Chapter 2.

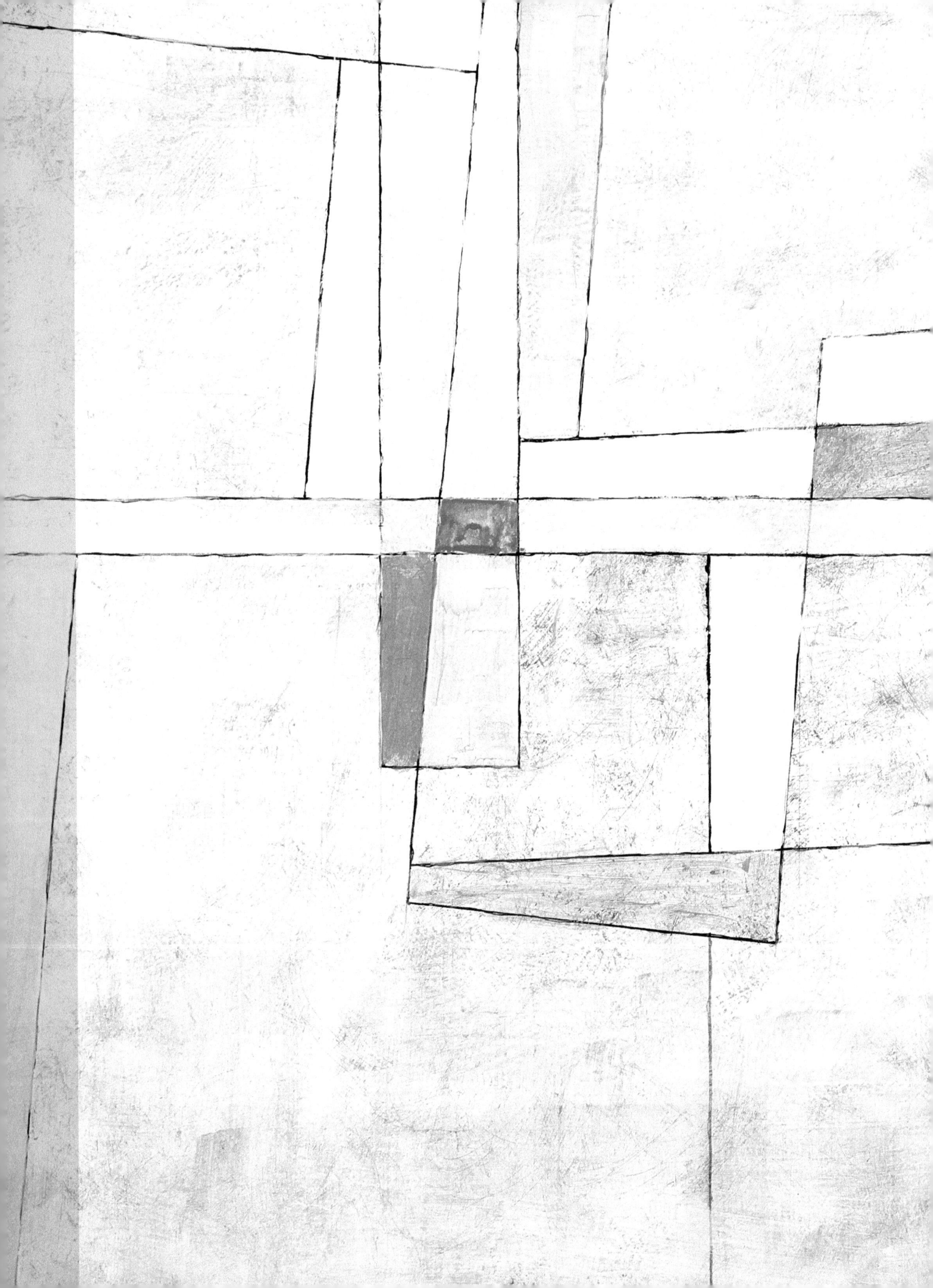

Introduction and Overview of Deliberate Practice and Motivational Interviewing

As I (J. K. M.) sat on a wooden chair, in a basement classroom at the University of New Mexico, I listened carefully as Dr. William Miller (Bill), my graduate school mentor, described the foundational principles of motivational interviewing (MI) to my class of first-year clinical psychology graduate students. An eager and driven student, I was intent on learning and becoming proficient in MI. I'd read Bill and Stephen Rollnick's text on MI and felt that the core concepts (open questions, affirmations, reflections, summary statements), were techniques that I already used in my everyday conversations. Suffice to say, I felt pretty confident in my MI skills. As the class shifted from lecture to role-play, I had the opportunity to practice my MI skills with a peer. My confidence in my MI skills waned as the role-play continued. Why did my reflections sound like questions? What if my reflections were wrong and I misunderstood what the client (my peer) was saying? As I stammered my way through the role-play, I found myself so concerned with what I was going to say next (should I reflect? ask an open-ended question?), that I realized I was barely attending to what my client was saying to me. As I left the class, I realized I'd greatly underestimated the complexity of MI.

Undeterred, I began looking for opportunities to practice my MI skills, particularly reflections, as I found those especially challenging. I offered reflections to the grocery clerk (e.g., "It's been a busy day for you"), my partner, neighbors, and family members. These interactions yielded mixed results. On occasion, my reflection was met with a puzzled look, and it was difficult for me to know if the bewilderment was because the grocery clerk wasn't used to an in-depth discussion on the busyness of the store or if my reflection had missed the mark.

Fortunately, my self-directed MI practice was complemented with training and supervision from Bill, along with Theresa Moyers (Terri), whom I regard as one of the most skilled MI clinicians in the world. Over time, as I practiced my MI skills and incorporated the feedback I received from Bill and Terri, I became comfortable in MI. I learned how to fully listen to my clients and offer compassion, while eliciting and reflecting language toward a particular target change. My expertise in MI has taken more than 20 years to develop, but in my early training years, I would have benefited from deliberate

https://doi.org/10.1037/0000297-001

Deliberate Practice in Motivational Interviewing, by J. K. Manuel, D. Ernst, A. Vaz, and T. Rousmaniere

practice, such as the structured exercises included in this book. These MI deliberate practice exercises are intended to elucidate the core techniques of MI as described in key MI texts (see the Required Reading in the sample syllabus in Appendix C). The repeated nature of the exercises is designed to increase comfort and proficiency in these core MI concepts, facilitating the transfer of these skills for use in clinical sessions with "real" clients.

As I grew in my comfort and skills as an MI clinician, I began to focus on effective MI training strategies. It became apparent that I was not alone in my early experiences of MI—to hold both a strong motivation to learn MI and an equally strong frustration with my struggle for mastery of the nuanced complexities of the approach. Research studies have demonstrated that learner confidence in their own MI skills often decreases after formalized training in the approach (Decker & Martino, 2013). This is consistent with the finding that MI learners often overestimate their MI skills before they are trained in the technique and underestimate their skills after they've received training (Hartzler et al., 2007). Deliberate practice can hone trainees' MI skills and foster realistic self-appraisal and confidence in the approach. Now that I've spent 20 years training others in MI, I am not surprised that trainees underestimate their MI skills after attending a workshop training. MI is a layered approach, consisting of foundational skills (e.g., open questions, reflections, affirmations) that seek to elicit and reinforce client language in favor of behavior change, while encapsulated in an overarching MI spirit. Having one without the others is not sufficient for the mastery of MI.

Overview of the Deliberate Practice Exercises

The main focus of the book is a series of 12 exercises that have been thoroughly tested and modified based on feedback from MI trainers and trainees. The 12 exercises represent essential MI skills. The last two exercises are more comprehensive, consisting of an annotated MI transcript and improvised mock MI sessions that teach clinicians how to integrate all these skills into more expansive clinical scenarios. Table 1.1 presents the 12 skills that are covered in these exercises.

Throughout all of the exercises, trainees work in pairs under the guidance of a supervisor and roleplay as a client and a clinician, switching back and forth between the two roles. Each of the 12 skill-focused exercises consists of multiple client statements grouped by difficulty—beginner, intermediate, and advanced—that call for a specific skill.

TABLE 1.1. The 12 Motivational Interviewing Skills Presented in the Deliberate Practice Exercises

Beginner Skills	Intermediate Skills	Advanced Skills
1. Simple reflections	5. Eliciting change talk	9. Simple and complex affirmations
2. Complex reflections, part 1: guesses at what the client means	6. Reflecting change talk	10. Autonomy support
	7. Double-sided reflections	11. Agenda mapping
3. Complex reflections, part 2: guesses at underlying client emotions or values	8. Dancing with discord	12. Elicit–provide–elicit
4. Reflections and open-ended questions		

For each skill, trainees are asked to read through and absorb the description of the skill, its criteria, and some examples of it. The trainee playing the client then reads the statements. The trainee playing the clinician then responds in a way that demonstrates the appropriate skill. Trainee clinicians will have the option of practicing a response using the one supplied in the exercise or immediately improvising and supplying their own.

After each client statement and clinician response couplet is practiced several times, the trainees will stop to receive feedback from the supervisor. Guided by the supervisor, the trainees will be instructed to try statement–response couplets several times, working their way down the list. In consultation with the supervisor, trainees will go through the exercises, starting with the least challenging and moving through to more advanced levels. The triad (supervisor–client–clinician) will have the opportunity to discuss whether exercises present too much or too little challenge and adjust up or down depending on the assessment. Trainees, in consultation with supervisors, can decide which skills they wish to work on and for how long. Based on our testing experience, we have found practice sessions last about 1 to 1.25 hours to receive maximum benefit. After this, trainees become saturated and need a break.

Ideally, MI learners will both gain confidence and achieve competence by practicing these exercises. Competence is defined here as the ability to perform an MI skill in a manner that aligns with the spirit of MI and is responsive to the client. Skills chosen for this book are considered essential to MI and often require practice and feedback.

The skills identified here are not comprehensive in the sense of representing all one needs to learn to become a competent MI clinician. Some will present particular challenges for trainees. A short history of MI and a brief description of the deliberate practice methodology are provided to explain how we have arrived at the union between them.

Goals of This Book

The primary goal of this book is to help trainees achieve competence in core MI skills.
The MI deliberate practice exercises are designed to accomplish the following:

1. Provide clinicians with the foundational skills of MI.

2. Help clinicians develop the ability to apply MI skills in a range of clinical situations (e.g., with varying levels of client ambivalence, a variety of target behaviors).

3. Move the skills into procedural memory (Squire, 2004) so that clinicians can access them even when they are tired, stressed, overwhelmed, or discouraged.

4. Provide MI clinicians in training with an opportunity to exercise the particular skill using a style and language that is congruent with who they are.

5. Provide the opportunity to use the MI skills in response to varying client statements and motivation to engage in a particular behavior change. This is designed to build confidence to adopt skills in a broad range of circumstances within different client contexts.

6. Provide clinicians in training with many opportunities to fail and then correct their failed response on the basis of feedback. This helps build confidence and persistence.

7. Finally, this book aims to help trainees discover their own personal learning style so they can continue their professional development long after their formal training is concluded.

Who Can Benefit From This Book?

This book is designed to be used in multiple contexts, including in graduate-level courses, supervision, postgraduate training, medical training, and other continuing education programs. It assumes the following:

1. The trainer is knowledgeable about and familiar with MI.

2. The trainer is able to provide good demonstrations of how to use MI skills across a range of clinical situations, via role-play, video, or both. Or, the trainer has access to examples of MI being demonstrated through the many MI video examples available (e.g., the series by Miller, Moyers, & Rollnick, n.d.; see https://www.changecompanies.net/products/motivational-interviewing-videos/).

3. The trainer is able to provide feedback to students regarding how to improve their MI skills.

4. Trainees will have accompanying reading, such as books and articles, that explain the theory, research, and rationale of MI and each particular skill. Recommended reading for each skill is provided in the sample syllabus (Appendix C).

The exercises covered in this book were piloted in 20 training sites from across three continents (North America, Europe, and Australia). Some training sites chose to translate the exercises into their native language to adopt them for use with their trainees. This book is designed for trainers and trainees from different cultural backgrounds worldwide.

This book is also designed for those who are training at all career stages, from beginning trainees, including those who have never worked with real clients, to seasoned clinicians. All exercises feature guidance for adjusting the difficulty to precisely target the needs of each individual learner. The term *trainee* in this book is used broadly, referring to anyone who is endeavoring to acquire MI skills.

Deliberate Practice in Clinical Training

How does one become an expert in their professional field? What is trainable, and what is simply beyond our reach, due to innate or uncontrollable factors? Questions such as these touch on our fascination with expert performers and their development. A mixture of awe, admiration, and even confusion surround people such as Mozart, Leonardo da Vinci, or more contemporary top performers such as basketball legend Michael Jordan and chess virtuoso Garry Kasparov. What accounts for their consistently superior professional results? Evidence suggests that the amount of or time spent on a particular type of training is a key factor in developing expertise in virtually all domains. "Deliberate practice" is an evidence-based method that can improve performance in an effective and reliable manner.

The concept of deliberate practice has its origins in a classic study by K. Anders Ericsson and colleagues (1993). They found that the amount of time practicing a skill and the quality of the time spent doing so were key factors predicting mastery and acquisition. They identified five key activities in learning and mastering skills: (a) observing one's own work; (b) getting expert feedback; (c) setting small, incremental learning goals just beyond the performer's ability; (d) engaging in repetitive behavioral rehearsal of specific skills; and (e) continuously assessing performance. Ericsson and his colleagues termed this process *deliberate practice*, a cyclical process that is illustrated in Figure 1.1.

FIGURE 1.1. Cycle of Deliberate Practice

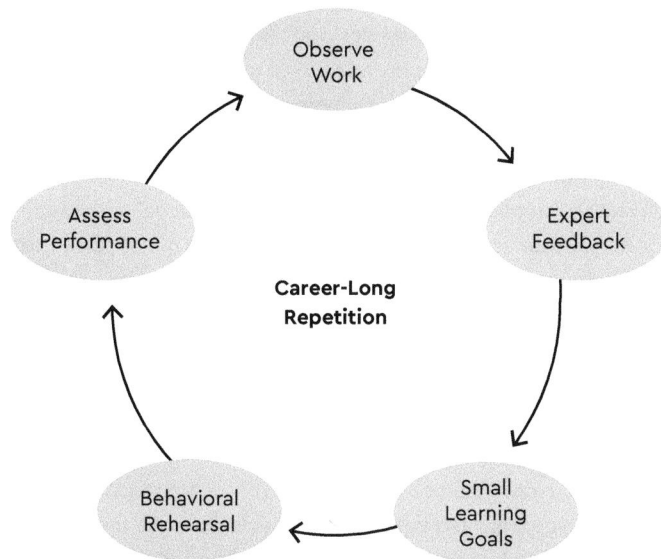

Note. From *Deliberate Practice in Emotion-Focused Therapy* (p. 7), by R. N. Goldman, A. Vaz, and T. Rousmaniere, 2021, American Psychological Association (https://doi.org/10.1037/0000227–000). Copyright 2021 by the American Psychological Association.

Research has shown that lengthy engagement in deliberate practice is associated with expert performance across a variety of professional fields, such as medicine, sports, music, chess, computer programming, and mathematics (Ericsson et al., 2018). People may associate deliberate practice with the widely known "10,000-hour rule" popularized by Malcolm Gladwell in his 2008 book *Outliers*, although the actual number of hours required for expertise varies by field and by individual (Ericsson & Pool, 2016). This, though, perpetuated two misunderstandings. First, that this is the number of deliberate practice hours that everyone needs to attain expertise, no matter the domain. In fact, there can be considerable variability in how many hours are required.

The second misunderstanding is that engagement in 10,000 hours of *work performance* will lead one to become an expert in that domain. This misunderstanding holds considerable significance for the field of psychotherapy and other clinical settings, where hours of work experience with clients has traditionally been used as a measure of proficiency (Rousmaniere, 2016). However, in fact, we know (Goldberg et al., 2016) that amount of experience alone does not predict clinician effectiveness. It may be that the *quality* of deliberate practice is a key factor. In addition, experience without feedback is like learning a new sport without a coach or team members. Feedback is essential in the acquisition of clinical skills and should be regarded as a key component in quality training.

Scholars, recognizing the value of deliberate practice in other fields, have recently called for deliberate practice to be incorporated into training for health care professionals (e.g., Bailey & Ogles, 2019; Hill et al., 2020; Rousmaniere et al., 2017; Taylor & Neimeyer, 2017; Tracey et al., 2015). There are, however, good reasons to question analogies made between clinical work, such as psychotherapy, and other professional fields, like sports or music, because by comparison clinical work is so complex and free form. Sports have clearly defined goals, and classical music follows a written score.

In contrast, the goals of clinical work shift with the unique presentation of each client in each clinical interaction. Clinicians do not have the luxury of following a score.

Instead, good MI is more like improvisational jazz (Noa Kageyama, cited in Rousmaniere, 2016). In jazz improvisations, a complex mixture of group collaboration, creativity, and interaction is coconstructed among band members. Like MI, no two jazz improvisations are identical. However, improvisations are not a random collection of notes. They are grounded in a comprehensive theoretical understanding and technical proficiency that is only developed through continuous deliberate practice. For example, prominent jazz instructor Jerry Coker listed 18 skill areas that students must master, each of which has multiple discrete skills, including tone quality, intervals, chord arpeggios, scales, patterns, and licks (Coker, 1990). In this sense, more creative and artful improvisations are actually a reflection of a previous commitment to repetitive skill practice and acquisition. As legendary jazz musician Miles Davis put it, "You have to play a long time to be able to play like yourself" (Cook, 2005).

The main idea that we would like to stress here is that we want deliberate practice to help MI clinicians become themselves. The idea is to learn the skills so that you have them on hand when you want them. Practice the skills to make them your own. Incorporate those aspects that feel right for you. Ongoing and effortful deliberate practice should not be an impediment to flexibility and creativity. Ideally, it should enhance it. We recognize and celebrate that clinical work is an ever-shifting encounter and by no means want it to become or feel formulaic. Strong MI clinicians mix an eloquent integration of previously acquired skills with properly attuned flexibility. The core MI responses provided are meant as templates or possibilities, rather than "answers." Please interpret and apply them as you see fit, in a way that makes sense to you.

Simulation-Based Mastery Learning

Deliberate practice uses simulation-based mastery learning (Ericsson, 2004; McGaghie et al., 2014). That is, the stimulus material for training consists of "contrived social situations that mimic problems, events, or conditions that arise in professional encounters" (McGaghie et al., 2014, p. 375). A key component of this approach is that the stimuli being used in training are sufficiently similar to real-world experiences. This facilitates *state-dependent learning*, in which professionals acquire skills in the same clinical environment where they will have to perform them (Fisher & Craik, 1977; Smith, 1979). For example, pilots train with flight simulators that present mechanical failures and dangerous weather conditions, and surgeons practice with surgical simulators that present medical complications. Training in simulations with challenging stimuli increases professionals' capacity to perform effectively under stress. For the MI training exercises in this book, the "simulators" are typical client statements that might actually be presented in the course of MI interactions and call upon the use of the particular MI skill.

Declarative Versus Procedural Knowledge

Declarative knowledge is what a person can understand, write, or speak about. It often refers to factual information that can be consciously recalled through memory and often acquired relatively quickly. In contrast, procedural learning is implicit in memory and "usually requires *repetition of an activity*, and associated learning is demonstrated through *improved task performance*" (Koziol & Budding, 2012, p. 2694, emphasis added). *Procedural knowledge* is what a person can perform, especially under stress (Squire, 2004). There can be a wide difference between their declarative and procedural knowledge.

For example, an "armchair quarterback" is a person who understands and talks about athletics well but would have trouble performing it at a professional level. Likewise, most dance, music, or theater critics have a very high ability to write about their subjects but would be flummoxed if asked to perform them.

In MI training, the gap between declarative and procedural knowledge appears when a trainee or clinician can speak about the theory of MI, such as the importance of reflective listening, but is unable to generate reflective listening statements in their own practice. They can speak to the "why" of reflective listening but can't offer the "how." **The sweet spot for deliberate practice is the gap between declarative and procedural knowledge.** In other words, effortful practice should target those skills that the trainee could write a good paper about but would have trouble actually performing with a real client. We start with declarative knowledge, learning skills theoretically and observing others perform them. Once learned, with the help of deliberate practice, we work toward the development of procedural learning, with the aim of clinicians having "automatic" access to each of the skills that they can pull on when necessary.

Let us turn to the theory of MI to help contextualize the skills of the book and how they fit into the greater training model.

Motivational Interviewing

MI was developed by Dr. William Miller (Bill) in the early 1980s. The approach grew out of Bill's clinical work in substance use treatment settings and was a stark alternative to the confrontational approach that prevailed in substance use treatment clinics at the time. MI continued to evolve as Bill began to collaborate with Dr. Stephen Rollnick, an early adopter of the approach. Together, they published the first MI text (Miller & Rollnick, 1991) and subsequent updated MI texts (Miller & Rollnick, 2002, 2013).

In the years since, MI has been widely disseminated, both in the United States and internationally. Hundreds of research trials have evaluated the efficacy of MI (e.g., Lundahl & Burke, 2009; Rubak et al., 2005) and found that it's effective as both a stand-alone treatment and in combination with other treatment modalities. Although the approach was originally developed for use with clients with alcohol or drug use disorders, its application and reach has expanded to include a variety of target behaviors (e.g., exercise, treatment adherence, vaccine acceptance, healthy eating). MI is often used in mental health, medical, criminal justice, and educational settings. It can be used as a starting point (i.e., Session 1) for other treatment modalities (Forman & Moyers, 2019) and in combination with other treatments to help build motivation for engagement in a longer duration of treatment, such as contingency management (Sayegh et al., 2017) and cognitive behavior therapy (CBT; Randall & McNeil, 2017).

Briefly stated, MI is a communication method (Miller & Rollnick, 2013) designed to elicit and strengthen a client's own reasons for engaging in a behavior change. It is client-centered yet directive and most appropriate with clients who are ambivalent about a behavior change. MI is intended to be brief, with interactions ranging from a few minutes to several sessions, depending on the clinical setting, the client's readiness and confidence to engage in a behavior change, and the complexity of the targeted change.

In sum, MI has a strong evidence base for use with a variety of target behaviors and across a range of clinical settings and populations. MI's popularity is likely due, in part, to the flexibility of the approach. It is client centered, so the principles and values of the approach apply broadly, regardless of the particular client situation. MI also fills a treatment gap. There are numerous well-studied treatment interventions for clients who are ready to engage in behavior change. Take smoking cessation as an example. Smoking cessation is widely studied, and there are a number of evidence-based approaches designed to help a person quit smoking (e.g., varenicline, lozenges, CBT). If a client mentions to a health care provider that they would like to quit smoking, the health care provider has an array of options to present to the client. In these cases, when the client is ready to quit smoking, MI strategies can be used to further strengthen the client's commitment to the change (e.g., "What are the benefits of quitting smoking for you? How might your life be different in a year, after you've quit smoking?"), but MI was developed and is intended for use with clients who are ambivalent about a behavior change—in this example, quitting smoking. A client who is ambivalent about quitting smoking may say something like, "Yeah, I should quit smoking. I've tried to quit a dozen times. It never works. I know it's bad for me. I know it will probably kill me and I'm spending a ton of money on it. I just keep doing it. I smoke and I don't even know I am smoking these days. It's part of me." This type of example can leave a clinician scratching their head about what to say next. Knowing MI fills this gap, helping bridge an ambivalent client to further treatment options, when indicated. It also takes the onus for a client's behavior change off of the clinician, perhaps one of the reasons why MI training is associated with decreased clinician burnout (Pollak et al., 2016). In MI, clinicians view clients as the experts on themselves. A clinician is there to guide, elicit, and reinforce steps toward behavior change, but the clinician either explicitly or implicitly acknowledges that the clinician cannot force a client to change their behavior.

As we move into the next section and discuss clinician empathy and MI spirit, we ask you to pause for a moment. Identify a behavior change you have considered making. Perhaps you have been thinking about eating less sugar, drinking less alcohol, getting more sleep, or adding exercise into your routine. How would you feel if someone told you the top five reasons you should make this change? Would they fit for you? What if they told you how you should implement this change? You may have felt some resistance, perhaps wanting to explain why this change was hard to make, why you haven't been able to do it, or why you don't want to do it. This reaction, to push back, is what we expect based on MI theory. The more a clinician pushes an ambivalent client toward a particular behavior change, the more the client is likely to push back. The more the client pushes back during an MI interaction, the less likely they are to engage in behavior change.

If we consider the behaviors that are most applicable for MI in clinical and research settings (e.g., smoking, drinking alcohol, sleep, using condoms), there are likely longstanding reasons clients want both to change and to remain the same. If we return to our smoking example, the client is offering us both reasons to quit smoking and reasons to continue to smoke. They are stuck. They may also feel some shame. Perhaps they've been told to quit smoking countless times by health care providers, friends, or family members. They may anticipate the discussion and feel defensive before the subject is even raised. In MI, it is essential that clinicians meet clients with empathy, to convey understanding to the client. This doesn't mean that the clinician must share the client's experiences or sympathize with the client. Rather, the clinician should listen to the client, hear what the client is saying, and offer that understanding back to the client. This often occurs through reflective listening, but empathy can occur in myriad ways.

MI spirit refers to a "way of being" with a client. It may feel very natural to some clinicians; for others, it may take a period of sustained practice before it feels comfortable. There are four main aspects of MI spirit: collaboration, acceptance, evocation, and compassion. *Collaboration* refers to the shared partnership between a clinician and client. The MI clinician is there to guide, but the client is truly viewed as the expert on themselves. The MI clinician respects the client's autonomy in their decision-making process. *Acceptance* refers to the nonjudgmental stance that is crucial in MI. The clinician may internally disagree with the client's behavior (e.g., a client who is drinking and driving) and, at the same time, accepts the client for who they are. *Evocation* refers to a clinician's deliberate efforts to elicit the client's perspective, their ideas, and thoughts on behavior change. Finally, *compassion* refers to the warmth and support that is offered to a client in MI interactions.

The role of client language is central to MI. Evaluations of MI sessions using standardized behavioral coding systems have revealed a relationship between client language and subsequent treatment outcomes. In MI, client language is categorized broadly into change talk and sustain talk. Client *change talk* includes language moving toward a specific behavioral change. It includes reasons ("I am spending too much money on cigarettes"), desire ("I really want to quit smoking"), ability ("I think I can quit if I use smoking lozenges"), need ("I need to quit once and for all"), commitment ("Monday is my quit day"), and taking steps ("I've bought some nicotine lozenges to help with the cravings"). Observational evaluations of MI sessions have demonstrated a positive association between client change talk and improved treatment outcomes. A stronger relationship exists between client *sustain talk*, or language moving away from change, and poorer treatment outcomes. Client sustain talk includes the following categories: reasons ("I like taking smoke breaks with my friends at work"), desire ("I don't want to quit smoking"), ability ("I've never been able to quit; it's impossible"), need ("I don't need to cut back. My smoking is fine"), commitment ("I am never going to quit"), and taking steps ("I stopped using the patch") with a clear distinction in that the client is arguing to maintain the status quo (e.g., continue smoking).

In the deliberate practice exercises included in this text, we focus on building specific MI skills (e.g., open questions, reflections, affirmations, autonomy support statements), These MI skills are specific behaviors that you, as the clinician, can use in your work with clients. Mastery of these skills, however, does not equate to MI proficiency. They must be delivered within the spirit of MI to be considered MI. We strongly encourage all trainees also to read the theory of MI (e.g., Miller & Rollnick, 2013). It can't be stated enough that the use of MI techniques alone is not sufficient in MI. The techniques must be accompanied by the spirit of MI, the way of being and working with clients. The spirit of MI may be an easy shift for some and may be quite difficult for others. Some find that the spirit of MI does not align with their clinical framework. MI is not a one-size-fits-all approach. We encourage you to use this approach only if it feels right for you. The choice is yours.

MI Skills in Deliberate Practice

The MI skills described in this text represent the foundational concepts that are central in MI. The skills are a mix of the two critical elements of MI: a relational component and a technical component. The relational component refers to the client-centered, empathic, and accepting relationship between an MI clinician and client (e.g., reflective listening, autonomy support statements, affirmations, dancing with discord, agenda mapping). In MI, clinicians seek to create a collaborative and nonjudgmental partnership with clients in which clients feel free to openly discuss their thoughts about a behavior change. Additionally, clients are given the space to think through their thoughts on behavior change. It's a process whereby the clinician and client are learning and discovering the client's reasons and plans for behavior change together, in a collaborative manner. This discovery process requires the clinician to be directive and understanding. It requires the clinician to reflect and ask questions and also to leave space for the client to share their perspective. The relational component of MI also emphasizes the client's autonomy in the change process. Clients may be officially told "this decision is up to you" (i.e., autonomy support statements) or it may occur more subtly, as the clinician asks the client what would be helpful to discuss with regard to the behavior change (i.e., agenda mapping).

The technical component of MI refers to a discerning focus on client change language. Ambivalent clients will naturally offer both change and sustain talk. The presence of sustain talk is both normal and expected in conversations with clients who are ambivalent about behavior change. In MI, clinicians learn to differentially respond to client change talk with the goal of strengthening or deepening the client's change talk statements. Clinicians must balance moving the client toward behavior change while maintaining a collaborative and client-centered approach. This can be tricky because clinicians need to decide how much and when to attend to client change talk versus client sustain talk. Clients tend to offer more sustain talk early in an MI session. This makes sense if we think of behavior change from the client's perspective. A client may begin an MI interaction feeling defensive, apprehensive, and unsure of what to expect. They may want to make sure the clinician understands why they have engaged in the behavior and how hard it may be to change. Early on, a clinician will want to develop rapport, to make sure the client feels understood. Moving too fast toward behavior change can leave the client feeling pressured to change or misunderstood. As the MI interaction continues and the client offers more change talk, the clinician may start to give preferential attention to client change talk, perhaps only reflecting change talk or offering double-sided reflections that end in change talk. Every client is different, so there's no set formula on how long a clinician should develop rapport before focusing more exclusively on client change talk. Client language will let the clinician know if they've pushed too far: Clinicians will hear increased client sustain talk, indicating they likely have gotten ahead of the client in the change process. This doesn't mean the clinician has failed or that the potential for change is doomed. Rather, the clinician can use this as an opportunity to reflect the client's perspective or highlight the client's autonomy in the change process.

Categorizing MI Skills

We have included 12 MI deliberate practice exercises in this text, each of which focuses on an individual skill. They represent foundational MI skills but are not an exhaustive list of all MI skills and techniques. The first 10 exercises represent key MI skills (i.e., open questions, reflections, affirmations, and autonomy support statements). Exercises 11 and 12 build on the skills presented in the earlier exercises (i.e., agenda mapping, elicit–provide–elicit).

The MI Skills Presented in Exercises 1 Through 12

The exercises begin with reflective listening, an essential and foundational MI skill (Exercises 1–3). Reflections are used to convey empathy and to move the client closer toward behavior change. Exercises 1 through 3 offer an opportunity to build on the complexity of the reflections offered, with Exercise 1 focusing on simple reflections and Exercises 2 and 3 highlighting two types of complex reflections: guessing what a client statement means and guessing the emotion or value underlying that statement. As discussed in the exercises, a key part of reflections is how they are offered to clients. Take the following example: "You aren't concerned about your drinking." The way these six words are enunciated can make a world of difference in a clinical interaction. If said with an inflection, this is a question, asking the client for confirmation or a response. Said sternly or harshly, the words sound confrontational, perhaps argumentative or incredulous. Offered as a statement, the six words may convey empathy when offered as a reflection. Often, new MI learners intend to offer reflections but find it difficult to transition from question-asking to reflections. Either their reflections may sound like questions (with an inflection at the end), or they may add a question to the end of the reflection (e.g., "You're concerned about your drinking. Is that right?"). This is where feedback from an observer is critical, otherwise a learner may build skills (e.g., repeated questions instead of reflections) that are inconsistent with the MI approach. Additionally, repeated practice of reflections is an effective way to build or reinforce new skills. Exercise 4 combines reflections with open-ended questions. This combination can be used to convey empathy to a client, while also eliciting the client's perspective.

Exercises 5 through 7 are focused on client language. Numerous research trials have demonstrated the relationship between within-session language and subsequent treatment outcomes, highlighting the importance of eliciting and reinforcing client language toward change. Through these exercises, trainees will learn how to identify and differentially respond to client change language. Exercise 8 expands on relationship discord, an amplified form of client sustain talk. As described earlier, client discord is a key signal that clinicians have gotten ahead of their clients in the change process. If and when this occurs, clinicians can pause, reflect the client's resistance, and may even want to change their approach ("I think I've gotten ahead of you. This is your decision. Let's talk a little more about your thoughts about [insert behavior change target]").

This text also includes a focus on clinician affirmations (Exercise 9) and autonomy support statements (Exercise 10), often referred to as MI-adherent clinician behaviors. These skills are important in both reinforcing client movements toward behavior change (e.g., "You've really thought a lot about the ways to quit smoking") and can be used to increase client self-efficacy for behavior change, a predictor of successful treatment outcomes. Autonomy support statements explicitly highlight the client's power and role in the decision to make a behavior change. This can be particularly impactful as many clients feel pressured or coerced to make a behavior change.

Finally, Exercises 11 and 12 are specific techniques that clinicians can use to identify and define the target behavior (as described in agenda mapping), and Exercise 12 provides a concrete way for clinicians to provide information in an MI-adherent manner.

A Note About Vocal Tone, Facial Expression, and Body Posture

As noted earlier, MI clinicians should give special consideration to their tone of voice. Tone of voice differentiates whether a clinician's expression is a reflection, question, or confrontational. Similarly, clinician body language is another form of expression, and clinicians should consider whether their body language is consistent with their verbal expressions. In general, clinicians should appear open and curious (e.g., refrain from crossing arms and closing self in) while allowing the client the space to think and process the reaction. Eye contact norms vary, but clinicians should avoid holding an extended gaze with the client because this could feel forced or aggressive. Additionally, clinicians should pause in the conversation and create space for the client to respond to the clinician statement. If clinicians rush to fill the space (e.g., immediately asking a question after a reflection), they are not allowing the client the opportunity to offer their perspective. These pauses can be uncomfortable at first, especially if this is new to the clinician, but will often feel more comfortable to the clinician over time.

The Role of Deliberate Practice in MI Training

Evaluations of effective methods of training clinicians in MI have occurred for more than 20 years. A number of trials have examined the utility of workshop training and training enhancements (e.g., ongoing coaching and feedback) and, unsurprisingly, have indicated that there is a not a one-size-fits-all approach to effective MI training. Nonetheless, the training literature indicates that ongoing coaching, supervision, feedback, or a combination of these are necessary to prevent MI skill decay. Over time, a clinician may return to asking questions instead of reflections or may lose their focus on eliciting and enhancing client change language.

Additionally, deliberate practice exercises have always been a core part of MI training. During in-person workshop trainings, trainees will often offer reflection after reflection to "build their MI muscle." Additionally, exercises may intentionally artificially limit the range of clinician responses (e.g., only reflect or ask open questions) to increase clinician comfort with new MI skills.

MI learners should be knowledgeable about the theory of MI (Miller & Rollnick, 2013). For broader reading on clinician interpersonal skills, learners may want to read *Effective Psychotherapists* (Miller & Moyers, 2021). There are MI texts for specific populations, such as adolescents and young adults (Naar & Suarez, 2021), diabetes management (Steinberg & Miller, 2015), health care settings (Rollnick et al., 2007), court-mandated populations (Stinson & Clark, 2017), psychological problems (Arkowitz et al., 2017), and group settings (Wagner & Ingersoll, 2012). For further information on MI skills and for activities to deepen MI skills, learners may want to read *Motivational Interviewing for Mental Health Clinicians: A Toolkit for Skills Enhancement* (Frey & Hall, 2021) and *Building Motivational Interviewing Skills: A Practitioner Workbook* (Rosengren, 2017).

Overview of the Book's Structure

This book is organized into three parts. Part I contains this chapter and Chapter 2, which provides basic instructions on how to perform these exercises. We found through testing that providing too many instructions upfront overwhelmed trainers and trainees, and they ended up skipping past them as a result. Therefore, we kept these instructions as brief and simple as possible to focus only on the most essential information that trainers and trainees will need to get started with the exercises. Further guidelines for getting the most about deliberate practice are provided in Chapter 3, and additional instructions for monitoring and adjusting the difficulty of the exercises are provided in Appendix A. **Do not skip the instructions in Chapter 2, and be sure to read the additional guidelines and instructions in Chapter 3 and Appendix A once you are comfortable with the basic instructions.**

Part II contains the 12 skill-focused exercises, which are ordered on the basis of their difficulty: beginner, intermediate, and advanced (see Table 1.1). Each contains a brief overview of the exercise, example client–clinician interactions to help guide trainees, step-by-step instructions for conducting that exercise, and a list of criteria for mastering the relevant skill. The client statements and sample clinician responses are then presented, also organized by difficulty (beginner, intermediate, and advanced). The statements and responses are presented separately so that the trainee playing the clinician has more freedom to improvise responses without being influenced by the sample responses, which should only be turned to if the trainee has difficulty improvising their own responses. The last two exercises in Part II provide opportunities to practice the 12 skills within simulated MI interactions. Exercise 13 provides a sample MI session transcript in which the MI skills are used and clearly labeled, thereby demonstrating how they might flow together in an actual MI interaction. MI trainees are invited to run through the sample transcript with one playing the clinician and the other playing the client to get a feel for how a session might unfold. Exercise 14 provides suggestions for undertaking actual mock sessions, as well as client profiles ordered by difficulty (beginner, intermediate, and advanced) that trainees can be used for improvised role-plays.

Part III contains Chapter 3, which provides additional guidance for trainers and trainees. While Chapter 2 is more procedural, Chapter 3 covers big-picture issues. It highlights six key points for getting the most out of deliberate practice and learning from being in the roles of trainer, trainee, and observer. The importance of the trainer–trainee relationship and responsive communication is described.

Three appendixes conclude this book. Appendix A provides instructions for monitoring and adjusting the difficulty of each exercise as needed. It provides a Deliberate Practice Reaction Form for the trainee playing the clinician to complete to indicate whether the exercise is too easy or too difficult. Appendix B includes a Deliberate Practice Diary Form that can be used to during a training session's final evaluation to process the trainees' experiences, but its primary purpose is to provide trainees a format to explore and record their experiences while engaging in additional, between-session deliberate practice activities without the supervisor. Appendix C presents a sample syllabus demonstrating how the 12 skill-focused deliberate practice exercises and other support material can be integrated into a wider MI training course. Instructors may choose to modify the syllabus or pick elements of it to integrate into their own courses.

Downloadable versions of this book's appendixes, including a color version of the Deliberate Practice Reaction Form, can be found in the "Clinician and Practitioner Resources" tab at https://www.apa.org/pubs/books/deliberate-practice-motivational-interviewing.

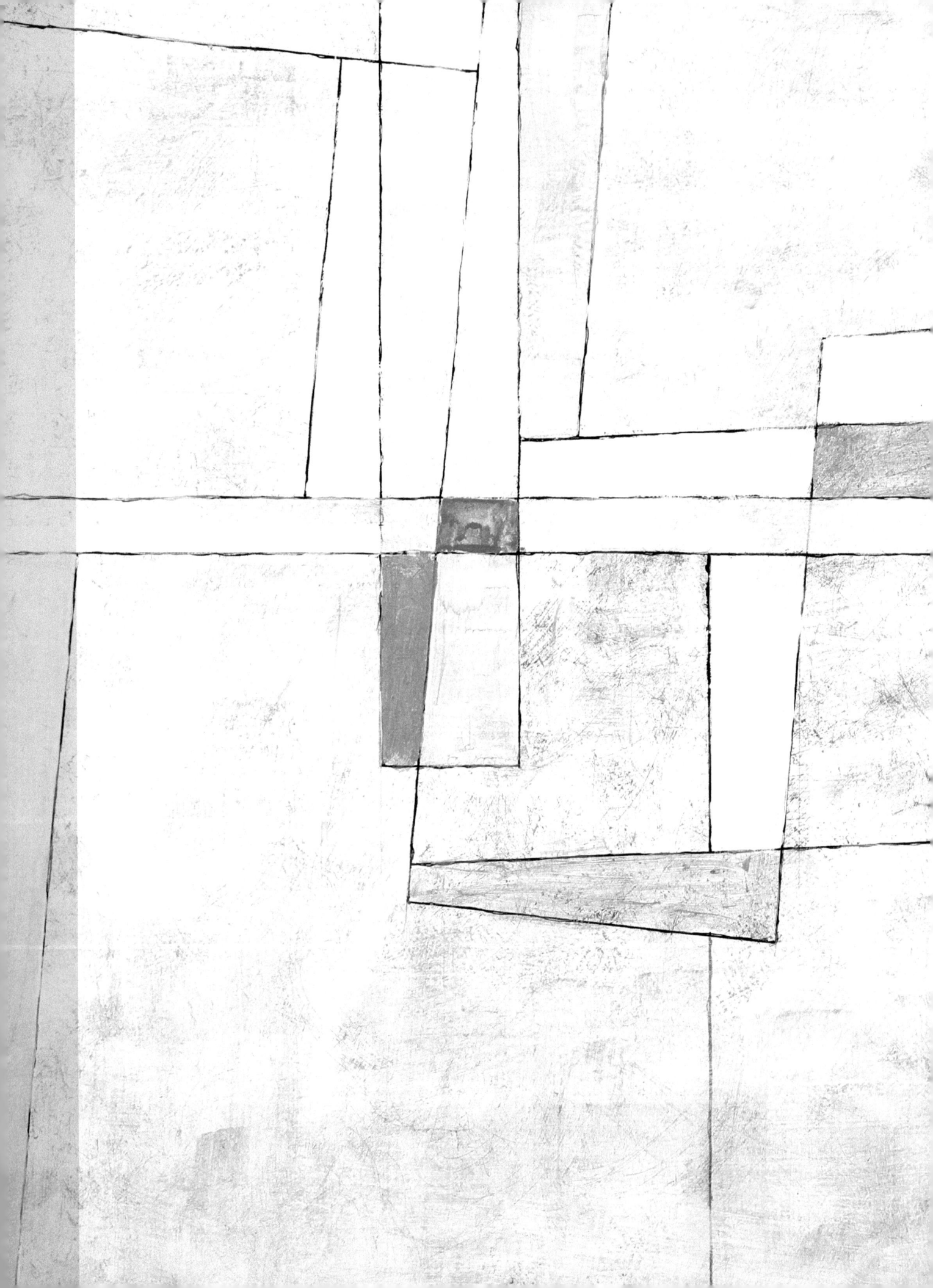

Instructions for the Motivational Interviewing Deliberate Practice Exercises

This chapter provides basic instructions that are common to all the exercises in this book. More specific instructions are provided in each exercise. Chapter 3 also provides important guidance for trainees and trainers that will help them get the most out of deliberate practice. Appendix A offers additional instructions for monitoring and adjusting the difficulty of the exercises as needed after getting through all then client statements in a single difficulty level, including a Deliberate Practice Reaction Form the trainee playing the clinician can complete to indicate whether they found the statements too easy or too difficult. **Difficulty assessment is an important part of the deliberate practice process and should not be skipped.**

Overview

The deliberate practice exercises in this book involve role-plays of hypothetical situations in a clinical interaction. The role-play involves three people: One trainee role-plays the clinician, another trainee role-plays the client, and a trainer (professor/supervisor) observes and provides feedback. Alternately, a peer can observe and provide feedback.

This book provides a script for each role-play, each with a client statement and also with an example clinician response. The client statements are graded in difficulty from beginning to advanced, although these difficulty grades are only estimates. The actual perceived difficulty of client statements is very subjective and varies widely by trainee. For example, some trainees may experience a stimulus of a client being angry to be easy to respond to, whereas another trainee may experience it as very difficult. Thus, it is important for trainees to provide difficulty assessments and adjustments to ensure that they are practicing at the right difficulty level: neither too easy nor too hard.

https://doi.org/10.1037/0000297-002

Deliberate Practice in Motivational Interviewing, by J. K. Manuel, D. Ernst, A. Vaz, and T. Rousmaniere

Time Frame

We recommend a 90-minute time block for every exercise, structured roughly as follows:

- First 20 minutes: Orientation. The trainer explains the motivational interviewing (MI) skill and demonstrates the exercise procedure with a volunteer trainee.

- Middle 50 minutes: Trainees perform the exercise in pairs. The trainer or a peer provides feedback throughout this process and monitors/adjusts the exercise's difficulty as needed after each set of statements (see Appendix A for more information about difficulty assessment).

- Final 20 minutes: Review, feedback, and discussion.

Preparation

1. Every trainee will need their own copy of this book.

2. Each exercise requires the trainer to fill out a Deliberate Practice Reaction Form after completing all the statements from a single difficulty level. The trainees should also complete a Deliberate Practice Diary Form during a training session's final evaluation and/or between sessions, particularly during additional deliberate practice activities. These forms are available at https://www.apa.org/pubs/books/deliberate-practice-motivational-interviewing (see the "Clinician and Practitioner Resources" tab) and in Appendixes A and B, respectively.

3. Trainees are grouped into pairs. One volunteers to role-play the clinician and one to role-play the client (they will switch roles after 15 minutes of practice). As noted previously, an observer who might be either the trainer or a fellow trainee will work with each pair.

The Role of the Trainer

The primary responsibilities of the trainer are as follows:

1. Observe the interaction and provide feedback, which includes both information about how well the trainees' response met expected criteria and any necessary guidance about how to improve the response.

2. Remind trainees to do difficulty assessments and adjustments after each level of client statements is completed (beginning, intermediate, and advanced).

How to Practice

Each exercise includes its own step-by-step instructions. Trainees should follow these instructions carefully because every step is important.

Skill Criteria

Each of the first 12 exercises focuses on one essential MI skill with two to four skill criteria that describe the important components or principles for that skill.

The goal of the role-play is for trainees to practice improvising responses to the client statement in a manner that (a) is attuned to the client, (b) meets skill criteria as much as possible, and (c) feels authentic for the trainee. Trainees are provided scripts with example clinician responses to give them a sense of how to incorporate the skill criteria into a response. **It is important, however, that trainees do not read the example responses verbatim in the role-plays!** MI interactions are highly personal and improvisational; the goal of deliberate practice is to develop trainees' ability to improvise within a consistent framework. Memorizing scripted responses would be counterproductive for helping trainees learn to perform interaction that is responsive, authentic, and attuned to each individual client.

Jennifer K. Manuel and Denise Ernst wrote the scripted example responses. However, trainees' personal style of interaction may differ slightly or greatly from that in the example scripts. It is essential that, over time, trainees develop their own style and voice, while simultaneously being able to stay client-centered and in the spirit of MI. To facilitate this, the exercises in this book were designed to maximize opportunities for improvisational responses informed by the skill criteria and ongoing feedback.

The goal for the role-plays is for trainees to practice improvising responses to the client statements in a manner that

- is attuned to the client,
- meets as many of the skill criteria as possible, and
- feels authentic for the trainee.

Review, Feedback, and Discussion

The review and feedback sequence after each role-play has these two elements:

- First, the trainee who played the client **briefly** shares how it felt to be on the receiving end of the clinician response. This can help assess how well trainees are attuning with the client.

- Second, the trainer provides **brief** feedback (less than 1 minute) based on the skill criteria for each exercise. Keep feedback specific, behavioral, brief, and MI-adherent (see Chapter 3) to preserve time for skill rehearsal. If one trainer is teaching multiple pairs of trainees, the trainer walks around the room, observing the pairs and offering brief feedback. When the trainer is not available, the trainee playing the client gives peer feedback to the clinician, based on the skill criteria and how it felt to be on the receiving end of the intervention. Alternatively, a third trainee can observe and provide feedback.

Trainers (or peers) should remember to keep all feedback specific and brief and not to veer into discussions of theory. There are many other settings for extended discussion of MI theory and research. In deliberate practice, it is of utmost importance to maximize time for continuous behavioral rehearsal via role-plays.

Final Evaluation

After both trainees have role-played the client and the clinician, the trainer provides an evaluation. Participants should engage in a short group discussion based on this evaluation. This discussion can provide ideas for where to focus homework and future deliberate practice sessions. To this end, Appendix B presents a Deliberate Practice Diary Form, which can also be downloaded from https://www.apa.org/pubs/books/deliberate-practice-motivational-interviewing (see the "Clinician and Practitioner Resources" tab). This form can be used as part of the final evaluation to help trainees process their experiences from that session with the supervisor. However, it is designed primarily to be used by trainees as a template for exploring and recording their thoughts and experiences between sessions, particularly when pursuing additional deliberate practice activities without the supervisor, such as rehearsing responses alone or if two trainees want practice the exercises together—perhaps with a third trainee filling the supervisor's role. Then, if they want, the trainees can discuss these experiences with the supervisor at the beginning of the next training session.

PART
II

Deliberate Practice Exercises for Motivational Interviewing Skills

This section of the book provides 12 deliberate practice exercises for essential motivational interviewing (MI) skills. These exercises are organized in a developmental sequence, from those that are more appropriate to someone just beginning MI training to those who have progressed to a more advanced level. Although we anticipate that most trainers would use these exercises in the order we have suggested, some trainers may find it more appropriate to their training circumstances to use a different order. We also provide two comprehensive exercises that bring together the MI skills using an annotated MI session transcript and mock MI sessions.

Exercises for Beginner Motivational Interviewing Skills

Exercises for Intermediate Motivational Interviewing Skills

Exercises for Advanced Motivational Interviewing Skills

Comprehensive Exercises

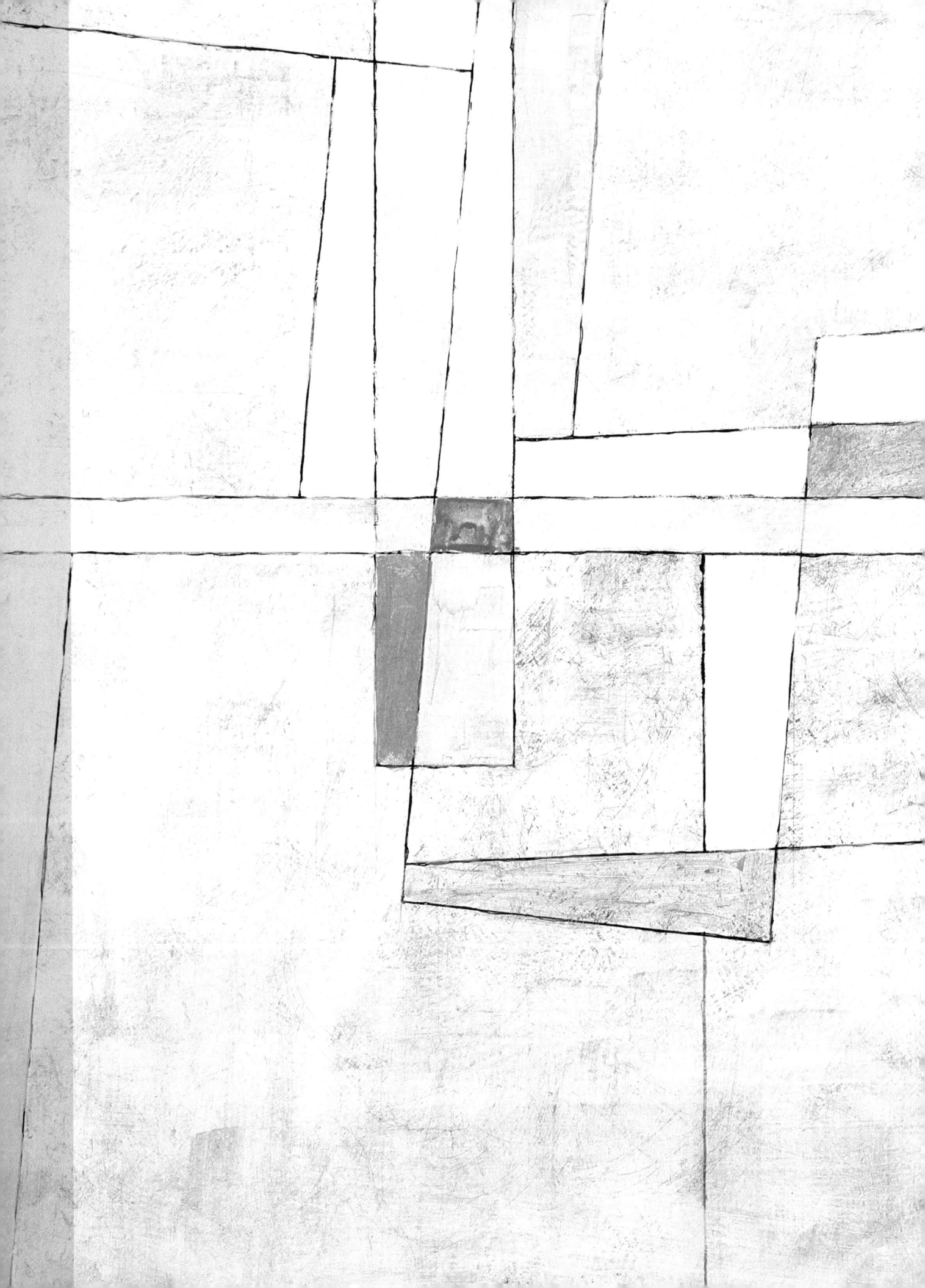

Simple Reflections

Preparations for Exercise 1

1. Read the instructions in Chapter 2.

2. Download the Deliberate Practice Reaction Form and the Deliberate Practice Diary Form at https://www.apa.org/pubs/books/deliberate-practice-motivational-interviewing (see the "Clinician and Practitioner Resources" tab; also available in Appendixes A and B, respectively).

Skill Description

Skill Difficulty Level: Beginner

Reflective listening is a key skill in motivational interviewing. Reflections are statements (not questions) that clinicians use to convey empathy and understanding to a client. Reflections are not interpretations, opinions, or advice. Reflections also vary in their complexity. Some reflections may repeat or rephrase what a client has stated. These are referred to as "Simple Reflections."

https://doi.org/10.1037/0000297-003

Deliberate Practice in Motivational Interviewing, by J. K. Manuel, D. Ernst, A. Vaz, and T. Rousmaniere

SKILL CRITERIA FOR EXERCISE 1
1. Reflections are offered as statements, not a question. There is no inflection at the end of the reflection.
2. Reflections follow and are connected to the client's statement.
3. The reflection does not include the clinician's opinion, advice, or information.
4. Simple reflections do not go beyond the client's statement or guess at any underlying meaning.

Examples of Clinicians Using Simple Reflections

Example 1

CLIENT: [*matter of fact*] My drinking has increased in the past year.

CLINICIAN: You're drinking more than you used to.

Example 2

CLIENT: [*concerned*] I'd like to exercise more. I hate the way I look and feel.

CLINICIAN: You aren't happy with the way you look and feel and you'd like to exercise more.

Example 3

CLIENT: [*frustrated*] I know I need to quit smoking. It's just so hard to do.

CLINICIAN: It's been hard to quit, and you know you need to do it.

Example 4

CLIENT: [*concerned*] My partner wants me to cut back on my drinking. He says it's out of control.

CLINICIAN: Your partner wants you to cut back.

INSTRUCTIONS FOR EXERCISE 1

Step 1: Role-Play and Feedback

- The client says the first beginner client statement. The clinician improvises a response based on the skill criteria.
- The trainer (or, if not available, the client) provides brief feedback based on the skill criteria.
- The client then repeats the same statement, and the clinician again improvises a response. The trainer (or client) again provides brief feedback.

Step 2: Repeat

- Repeat Step 1 for all the statements in the current difficulty level (beginner, intermediate, or advanced).

Step 3: Assess and Adjust Difficulty

- The clinician completes the Deliberate Practice Reaction Form (see Appendix A) and decides whether to make the exercise easier or harder or to repeat the same difficulty level.

Step 4: Repeat for Approximately 15 Minutes

- Repeat Steps 1 to 3 for at least 15 minutes.
- The trainees then switch clinician and client roles and start over.

Now it's your turn! Follow Steps 1 and 2 from the instructions.

Remember: The goal of the role-play is for trainees to practice improvising responses to the client statements in a manner that (a) uses the skill criteria and (b) feels authentic for the trainee. **Example clinician responses for each client statement are provided at the end of this exercise. Trainees should attempt to improvise their own responses before reading the example responses.**

BEGINNER-LEVEL CLIENT STATEMENTS FOR EXERCISE 1
Beginner Client Statement 1
[Matter of fact] I drink about a six-pack of beer a day.
Beginner Client Statement 2
[Sad] My kids really want me to quit smoking.
Beginner Client Statement 3
[Defensive] I like to drink. It's not a big deal.
Beginner Client Statement 4
[Concerned] I lose track of time on social media.
Beginner Client Statement 5
[Adamant] I should cut back on my sugar intake.

Assess and adjust the difficulty before moving to the next difficulty level (see Step 3 in the exercise instructions).

INTERMEDIATE-LEVEL CLIENT STATEMENTS FOR EXERCISE 1
Intermediate Client Statement 1
[Frustrated] I've smoked since I was 15 years old. I've never been able to quit.
Intermediate Client Statement 2
[Exasperated] All of my friends drink as much as I do.
Intermediate Client Statement 3
[Frustrated] I used to exercise more regularly. I just don't have time now.
Intermediate Client Statement 4
[Motivated] I should quit smoking. I know it's not good for me.
Intermediate Client Statement 5
[Hopeful] I felt better when I was eating more fruits and vegetables.

Assess and adjust the difficulty before moving to the next difficulty level (see Step 3 in the exercise instructions).

ADVANCED-LEVEL CLIENT STATEMENTS FOR EXERCISE 1
Advanced Client Statement 1
[Contemplative] I think it would be easier for me to exercise if I signed up for an exercise program.
Advanced Client Statement 2
[Slowly, with uncertainty] I've done some stupid things while drunk. And I've had a few blackouts but no legal troubles or anything like that.
Advanced Client Statement 3
[Frustrated] No one understands how hard it is to quit smoking. It's practically impossible.
Advanced Client Statement 4
[Concerned] I know I shouldn't be using my phone while driving.
Advanced Client Statement 5
[Matter of fact] I am not getting enough sleep. I start watching TV and can't pull myself away.

Assess and adjust the difficulty here (see Step 3 in the exercise instructions). If appropriate, follow the instructions to make the exercise even more challenging (see Appendix A).

Example Clinician Responses: Simple Reflections

Remember: Trainees should attempt to improvise their own responses before reading the example responses. **Do not read the following responses verbatim unless you are having trouble coming up with your own responses!**

EXAMPLE RESPONSES TO BEGINNER-LEVEL CLIENT STATEMENTS FOR EXERCISE 1
Example Response to Beginner Client Statement 1
You drink beer every day.
Example Response to Beginner Client Statement 2
Your kids want you to quit smoking.
Example Response to Beginner Client Statement 3
Drinking isn't a big deal to you.
Example Response to Beginner Client Statement 4
You get caught up in social media.
Example Response to Beginner Client Statement 5
Your sugar intake is too high right now.

EXAMPLE RESPONSES TO INTERMEDIATE-LEVEL CLIENT STATEMENTS FOR EXERCISE 1
Example Response to Intermediate Client Statement 1
You've been a smoker for a long time.
Example Response to Intermediate Client Statement 2
You're drinking the same amount as your friends.
Example Response to Intermediate Client Statement 3
You're busy.
Example Response to Intermediate Client Statement 4
You know you should quit smoking.
Example Response to Intermediate Client Statement 5
You felt healthier when you were eating fruits and vegetables.

EXAMPLE RESPONSES TO ADVANCED-LEVEL CLIENT STATEMENTS FOR EXERCISE 1
Example Response to Advanced Client Statement 1
An exercise program would make it easier to exercise.
Example Response to Advanced Client Statement 2
You haven't had any legal problems because of your drinking.
Example Response to Advanced Client Statement 3
Quitting smoking is hard.
Example Response to Advanced Client Statement 4
You know it's not a good idea to use your phone while driving.
Example Response to Advanced Client Statement 5
It's hard for you to pull yourself away from the TV at night.

Complex Reflections, Part 1: Guesses at What the Client Means

Preparations for Exercise 2

1. Read the instructions in Chapter 2.

2. Download the Deliberate Practice Reaction Form and the Deliberate Practice Diary Form at https://www.apa.org/pubs/books/deliberate-practice-motivational-interviewing (see the "Clinician and Practitioner Resources" tab; also available in Appendixes A and B, respectively).

Skill Description

Skill Difficulty Level: Beginner

Complex reflections, like simple reflections, convey empathy and understanding to a client. As their name describes, complex reflections are more elaborate reflections. They are richer, deeper reflections. Complex reflections are often a clinician's guess at the underlying meaning in a previous client statement. For example, a client may say, "I've never been able to quit smoking for more than a day." At first read, this sounds like a client who is frustrated with their past attempts to quit smoking. Other guesses at what the client may mean with this statement could include "you really want to quit smoking" or "you're tired of trying to quit smoking and don't want to even try again." Guesses that go beyond what a client has explicitly stated can often help the client (and the clinician) better understand the deeper meaning of the client's original statement. When a clinician is offering guesses in the form of reflections, they may not know if the client will agree with the reflection. The goal is for the clinician to convey empathy while collaboratively discovering the underlying meaning of the client's statements.

https://doi.org/10.1037/0000297-004
Deliberate Practice in Motivational Interviewing, by J. K. Manuel, D. Ernst, A. Vaz, and T. Rousmaniere

SKILL CRITERIA FOR EXERCISE 2

1. The clinician guesses at a deeper meaning in the client's words.
2. Reflections are offered as statements, not questions. There is no inflection at the end of the reflection.
3. The reflection does not include the clinician's opinion, advice, or information.

Examples of Clinicians Guessing What the Client Means

Example 1

CLIENT: [*matter of fact*] My drinking has increased in the past year.

CLINICIAN: You're really noticing a difference.

Example 2

CLIENT: [*concerned*] I'd like to exercise more. I hate the way I look and feel.

CLINICIAN: Your health is really important to you. You want to make a change.

Example 3

CLIENT: [*frustrated*] I know I need to quit smoking. It's just so hard to do.

CLINICIAN: You're fed up with smoking. You want to be done with it.

Example 4

CLIENT: [*concerned*] My partner wants me to cut back on my drinking. He says it's out of control.

CLINICIAN: This relationship is important to you. You don't want your drinking to impact it.

INSTRUCTIONS FOR EXERCISE 2
Step 1: Role-Play and Feedback
• The client says the first beginner client statement. The clinician improvises a response based on the skill criteria. • The trainer (or, if not available, the client) provides brief feedback based on the skill criteria. • The client then repeats the same statement, and the clinician again improvises a response. The trainer (or client) again provides brief feedback.
Step 2: Repeat
• Repeat Step 1 for all the statements in the current difficulty level (beginner, intermediate, or advanced).
Step 3: Assess and Adjust Difficulty
• The clinician completes the Deliberate Practice Reaction Form (see Appendix A) and decides whether to make the exercise easier or harder or to repeat the same difficulty level.
Step 4: Repeat for Approximately 15 Minutes
• Repeat Steps 1 to 3 for at least 15 minutes. • The trainees then switch clinician/client roles and start over.

Now it's your turn! Follow Steps 1 and 2 from the instructions.

Remember: The goal of the role-play is for trainees to practice improvising responses to the client statements in a manner that (a) uses the skill criteria and (b) feels authentic for the trainee. **Example clinician responses for each client statement are provided at the end of this exercise. Trainees should attempt to improvise their own responses before reading the example responses.**

BEGINNER-LEVEL CLIENT STATEMENTS FOR EXERCISE 2
Beginner Client Statement 1
[Matter of fact] I drink about a six-pack of beer a day.
Beginner Client Statement 2
[Sad] My kids really want me to quit smoking.
Beginner Client Statement 3
[Defensive] I like to drink. It's not a big deal.
Beginner Client Statement 4
[Concerned] I lose track of time on social media.
Beginner Client Statement 5
[Adamant] I should cut back on my sugar intake.

Assess and adjust the difficulty before moving to the next difficulty level (see Step 3 in the exercise instructions).

INTERMEDIATE-LEVEL CLIENT STATEMENTS FOR EXERCISE 2
Intermediate Client Statement 1
[Frustrated] I've smoked since I was 15 years old. I've never been able to quit.
Intermediate Client Statement 2
[Exasperated] All of my friends drink as much as I do.
Intermediate Client Statement 3
[Frustrated] I used to exercise more regularly. I just don't have time now.
Intermediate Client Statement 4
[Motivated] I should quit smoking. I know it's not good for me.
Intermediate Client Statement 5
[Hopeful] I felt better when I was eating more fruits and vegetables.

Assess and adjust the difficulty before moving to the next difficulty level (see Step 3 in the exercise instructions).

ADVANCED-LEVEL CLIENT STATEMENTS FOR EXERCISE 2
Advanced Client Statement 1
[Contemplative] I think it would be easier for me to exercise if I signed up for an exercise program.
Advanced Client Statement 2
[Slowly, with uncertainty] I've done some stupid things while drunk. And I've had a few blackouts but no legal troubles or anything like that.
Advanced Client Statement 3
[Frustrated] No one understands how hard it is to quit smoking. It's practically impossible.
Advanced Client Statement 4
[Concerned] I know I shouldn't be using my phone while driving.
Advanced Client Statement 5
[Matter of fact] I am not getting enough sleep. I start watching TV and can't pull myself away.

🖐 **Assess and adjust the difficulty here (see Step 3 in the exercise instructions). If appropriate, follow the instructions to make the exercise even more challenging (see Appendix A).**

Example Clinician Responses: Guesses at What the Client Means

Remember: Trainees should attempt to improvise their own responses before reading the example responses. **Do not read the following responses verbatim unless you are having trouble coming up with your own responses!**

EXAMPLE RESPONSES TO BEGINNER-LEVEL CLIENT STATEMENTS FOR EXERCISE 2
Example Response to Beginner Client Statement 1
Beer is a big part of your life.
Example Response to Beginner Client Statement 2
You want to be a good role model for your kids. They notice what you do.
Example Response to Beginner Client Statement 3
You don't see a reason to make any changes to your drinking.
Example Response to Beginner Client Statement 4
You've been surprised at how much time you're spending on social media.
Example Response to Beginner Client Statement 5
You're ready to make some changes to your sugar intake.

EXAMPLE RESPONSES TO INTERMEDIATE-LEVEL CLIENT STATEMENTS FOR EXERCISE 2
Example Response to Intermediate Client Statement 1
Smoking has been a big part of your life.
Example Response to Intermediate Client Statement 2
Drinking is a big part of your social life.
Example Response to Intermediate Client Statement 3
You've incorporated exercise into your life before.
Example Response to Intermediate Client Statement 4
It could be causing you some problems.
Example Response to Intermediate Client Statement 5
It's important for you to be healthy.

EXAMPLE RESPONSES TO ADVANCED-LEVEL CLIENT STATEMENTS FOR EXERCISE 2
Example Response to Advanced Client Statement 1
An exercise program is the first step toward feeling better.
Example Response to Advanced Client Statement 2
You're unsure about your drinking. It's not caused you legal problems, but there've been a few things that have happened that were troubling.
Example Response to Advanced Client Statement 3
You've felt alone in this process.
Example Response to Advanced Client Statement 4
Having the phone in the car is tempting. It's hard to ignore.
Example Response to Advanced Client Statement 5
Setting some limits with evening TV would help with your sleep.

Complex Reflections, Part 2: Guesses at Underlying Client Emotions or Values

Preparations for Exercise 3

1. Read the instructions in Chapter 2.

2. Download the Deliberate Practice Reaction Form and the Deliberate Practice Diary Form at https://www.apa.org/pubs/books/deliberate-practice-motivational-interviewing (see the "Clinician and Practitioner Resources" tab; also available in Appendixes A and B, respectively).

Skill Description

Skill Difficulty Level: Beginner

Another type of complex reflection is a guess at the underlying emotion or value expressed in a client statement. In this kind of complex reflection, the clinician is listening for emotions that are unexpressed or indirectly expressed in the client's statement. These can be impactful in motivational interviewing (MI) sessions because they often begin to reflect a client's values and the ways in which their actions (e.g., smoking, drinking) do not align with their values (e.g., to be healthy, a good parent/partner). Complete accuracy is not necessary when reflecting a client's emotions. Most clients will experience reflections as a clinician's attempts to understand their perspective and experiences, particularly if these exchanges occur within a collaborative and empathic interaction that is consistent with the MI approach.

https://doi.org/10.1037/0000297-005
Deliberate Practice in Motivational Interviewing, by J. K. Manuel, D. Ernst, A. Vaz, and T. Rousmaniere

SKILL CRITERIA FOR EXERCISE 3

1. The clinician guesses at the underlying emotion that the client has not directly stated.
2. Reflections are offered as statements, not questions. There is no inflection at the end of the reflection.
3. The reflection does not include the clinician's opinion, advice, or information.

Examples of Clinicians Guessing at Underlying Client Emotions or Values

Example 1

CLIENT: [*matter of fact*] My drinking has increased in the past year.

CLINICIAN: You're concerned about this increase in your drinking.

Example 2

CLIENT: [*concerned*] I'd like to exercise more. I hate the way I look and feel.

CLINICIAN: You're frustrated and want to change.

Example 3

CLIENT: [*frustrated*] I know I need to quit smoking. It's just so hard to do.

CLINICIAN: You're really motivated to quit.

Example 4

CLIENT: [*concerned*] My partner wants me to cut back on my drinking. He says it's out of control.

CLINICIAN: Your partner is worried and really cares about you.

INSTRUCTIONS FOR EXERCISE 3

Step 1: Role-Play and Feedback

- The client says the first beginner client statement. The clinician improvises a response based on the skill criteria.
- The trainer (or, if not available, the client) provides brief feedback based on the skill criteria.
- The client then repeats the same statement, and the clinician again improvises a response. The trainer (or client) again provides brief feedback.

Step 2: Repeat

- Repeat Step 1 for all the statements in the current difficulty level (beginner, intermediate, or advanced).

Step 3: Assess and Adjust Difficulty

- The clinician completes the Deliberate Practice Reaction Form (see Appendix A) and decides whether to make the exercise easier or harder or to repeat the same difficulty level.

Step 4: Repeat for Approximately 15 Minutes

- Repeat Steps 1 to 3 for at least 15 minutes.
- The trainees then switch therapist and client roles and start over.

> **Now it's your turn! Follow Steps 1 and 2 from the instructions.**

Remember: The goal of the role-play is for trainees to practice improvising responses to the client statements in a manner that (a) uses the skill criteria and (b) feels authentic for the trainee. **Example clinician responses for each client statement are provided at the end of this exercise. Trainees should attempt to improvise their own responses before reading the example responses.**

BEGINNER-LEVEL CLIENT STATEMENTS FOR EXERCISE 3
Beginner Client Statement 1
[Matter of fact] I drink about a six-pack of beer a day.
Beginner Client Statement 2
[Sad] My kids really want me to quit smoking.
Beginner Client Statement 3
[Defensive] I like to drink. It's not a big deal.
Beginner Client Statement 4
[Concerned] I lose track of time on social media.
Beginner Client Statement 5
[Adamant] I should cut back on my sugar intake.

> **Assess and adjust the difficulty before moving to the next difficulty level (see Step 3 in the exercise instructions).**

INTERMEDIATE-LEVEL CLIENT STATEMENTS FOR EXERCISE 3
Intermediate Client Statement 1
[Frustrated] I've smoked since I was 15 years old. I've never been able to quit.
Intermediate Client Statement 2
[Exasperated] All of my friends drink as much as I do.
Intermediate Client Statement 3
[Frustrated] I used to exercise more regularly. I just don't have time now.
Intermediate Client Statement 4
[Motivated] I should quit smoking. I know it's not good for me.
Intermediate Client Statement 5
[Hopeful] I felt better when I was eating more fruits and vegetables.

Assess and adjust the difficulty before moving to the next difficulty level (see Step 3 in the exercise instructions).

ADVANCED-LEVEL CLIENT STATEMENTS FOR EXERCISE 3
Advanced Client Statement 1
[Contemplative] I think it would be easier for me to exercise if I signed up for an exercise program.
Advanced Client Statement 2
[Slowly, with uncertainty] I've done some stupid things while drunk. And I've had a few blackouts but no legal troubles or anything like that.
Advanced Client Statement 3
[Frustrated] No one understands how hard it is to quit smoking. It's practically impossible.
Advanced Client Statement 4
[Concerned] I know I shouldn't be using my phone while driving.
Advanced Client Statement 5
[Matter of fact] I am not getting enough sleep. I start watching TV and can't pull myself away.

✋ **Assess and adjust the difficulty here (see Step 3 in the exercise instructions). If appropriate, follow the instructions to make the exercise even more challenging (see Appendix A).**

Example Clinician Responses: Guesses at Underlying Client Emotions or Values

Remember: Trainees should attempt to improvise their own responses before reading the example responses. **Do not read the following responses verbatim unless you are having trouble coming up with your own responses!**

EXAMPLE RESPONSES TO BEGINNER-LEVEL CLIENT STATEMENTS FOR EXERCISE 3
Example Response to Beginner Client Statement 1
You're worried about your drinking.
Example Response to Beginner Client Statement 2
They're concerned about your health.
Example Response to Beginner Client Statement 3
Drinking is a big part of your life. You enjoy it.
Example Response to Beginner Client Statement 4
You're concerned that you're spending too much time on social media.
Example Response to Beginner Client Statement 5
Your health is important to you and you are ready to cut back on your sugar intake.

EXAMPLE RESPONSES TO INTERMEDIATE-LEVEL CLIENT STATEMENTS FOR EXERCISE 3
Example Response to Intermediate Client Statement 1
You're frustrated that you haven't been able to successfully quit smoking yet.
Example Response to Intermediate Client Statement 2
You enjoy drinking with your friends.
Example Response to Intermediate Client Statement 3
It's frustrating. You'd like to exercise more.
Example Response to Intermediate Client Statement 4
You worry what might happen if you continue to smoke.
Example Response to Intermediate Client Statement 5
You can appreciate the changes you feel when eating healthier.

EXAMPLE RESPONSES TO ADVANCED-LEVEL CLIENT STATEMENTS FOR EXERCISE 3
Example Response to Advanced Client Statement 1
You want to exercise more and are optimistic that an exercise program will help.
Example Response to Advanced Client Statement 2
You feel some regret about your drinking.
Example Response to Advanced Client Statement 3
It's been frustrating. You really want to quit smoking.
Example Response to Advanced Client Statement 4
You worry about what might happen.
Example Response to Advanced Client Statement 5
You're exhausted and know the late-night TV is causing some problems.

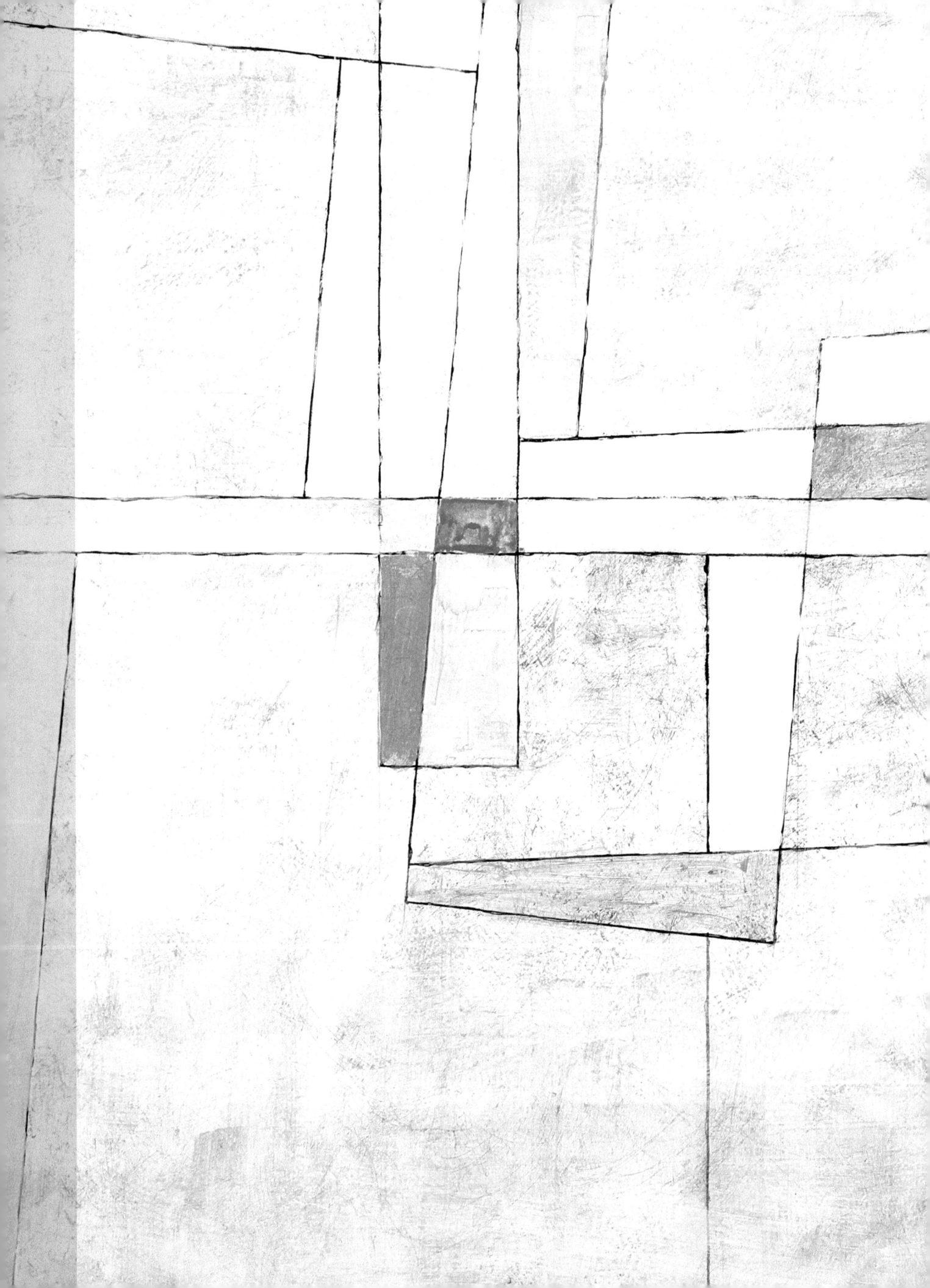

Reflections and Open-Ended Questions

Preparations for Exercise 4

1. Read the instructions in Chapter 2.

2. Download the Deliberate Practice Reaction Form and the Deliberate Practice Diary Form at https://www.apa.org/pubs/books/deliberate-practice-motivational-interviewing (see the "Clinician and Practitioner Resources" tab; also available in Appendixes A and B, respectively).

Skill Description

Skill Difficulty Level: Beginner

Open-ended questions are used in motivational interviewing (MI) interactions to elicit a client's perspective and to move the conversation along. Open-ended questions often begin with "what," "why," or "how" and elicit a longer response from clients, whereas closed questions allow for a one or two-word response, such as "yes" or "no." Open-ended questions provide the client the opportunity to share their thoughts, ideas, and strategies about a specific behavioral change.

While open-ended questions can be effective in eliciting client change talk or a client's thoughts, they should be used in combination with other MI techniques (e.g., reflections, affirmations). Novice MI clinicians should aim to offer approximately the same number of questions and reflections in an MI interaction, while advanced MI clinicians should aim to offer twice as many reflections as questions.

https://doi.org/10.1037/0000297–006

Deliberate Practice in Motivational Interviewing, by J. K. Manuel, D. Ernst, A. Vaz, and T. Rousmaniere

SKILL CRITERIA FOR EXERCISE 4
1. The clinician responds to the client statement with a *reflection* followed by an *open-ended question*.
2. The reflection can be either simple or complex, as described in Exercises 1 through 3.
3. Remember that open-ended questions encourage more than a one-word response and often begin with "what," "why," or "how."

Examples of Clinicians Responding With a Reflection and an Open-Ended Question

Example 1

CLIENT: [*thoughtful*] I'm not sure vaping is good for me.

CLINICIAN: You're not sure what vaping might be doing to you. (Reflection) What concerns do you have about vaping? (Open-Ended Question)

Example 2

CLIENT: [*matter of fact*] I haven't vaped for a long time.

CLINICIAN: You've taken a break from vaping. (Reflection) What are your thoughts about vaping? (Open-Ended Question)

Example 3

CLIENT: [*frustrated*] My partner wants me to cut back on my drinking.

CLINICIAN: Your partner has some thoughts about your drinking. (Reflection) How would you like things to be different with your drinking? (Open-Ended Question)

Example 4

CLIENT: [*matter of fact*] I might want to cut back sometime.

CLINICIAN: You may cut back at some point. (Reflection) What are your thoughts about if and when you might make a change in your drinking? (Open-Ended Question)

Example 5

CLIENT: [*concerned*] My drinking has gotten a bit worse in the last year.

CLINICIAN: You're noticing a change in your drinking. (Reflection) How has drinking affected your life? (Open-Ended Question)

INSTRUCTIONS FOR EXERCISE 4

Step 1: Role-Play and Feedback

- The client says the first beginner client statement. The clinician improvises a response based on the skill criteria.
- The trainer (or, if not available, the client) provides brief feedback based on the skill criteria.
- The client then repeats the same statement, and the clinician again improvises a response. The trainer (or client) again provides brief feedback.

Step 2: Repeat

- Repeat Step 1 for all the statements in the current difficulty level (beginner, intermediate, or advanced).

Step 3: Assess and Adjust Difficulty

- The clinician completes the Deliberate Practice Reaction Form (see Appendix A) and decides whether to make the exercise easier or harder or to repeat the same difficulty level.

Step 4: Repeat for Approximately 15 Minutes

- Repeat Steps 1 to 3 for at least 15 minutes.
- The trainees then switch clinician and client roles and start over.

Now it's your turn! Follow Steps 1 and 2 from the instructions.

Remember: The goal of the role-play is for trainees to practice improvising responses to the client statements in a manner that (a) uses the skill criteria and (b) feels authentic for the trainee. **Example clinician responses for each client statement are provided at the end of this exercise. Trainees should attempt to improvise their own responses before reading the example responses.**

BEGINNER-LEVEL CLIENT STATEMENTS FOR EXERCISE 4
Beginner Client Statement 1
[Matter of fact] My doctor wanted me to talk to you about my drinking.
Beginner Client Statement 2
[Thoughtful] I think it's probably time for me to cut back on my cannabis use.
Beginner Client Statement 3
[Concerned] My friends think I need to go to treatment.
Beginner Client Statement 4
[Concerned] I should try to get more sleep at night.
Beginner Client Statement 5
[Confident] I've done this before. I can do it again.

Assess and adjust the difficulty before moving to the next difficulty level (see Step 3 in the exercise instructions).

INTERMEDIATE-LEVEL CLIENT STATEMENTS FOR EXERCISE 4
Intermediate Client Statement 1
[Matter of fact] I'm not worried about my cannabis use, but my friends have made some comments.
Intermediate Client Statement 2
[Unconcerned] I know my drinking has increased lately.
Intermediate Client Statement 3
[Concerned] The cravings are tough. I can't quit without something to help with the cravings.
Intermediate Client Statement 4
[Sad] I'm here to get help with my pain pills.
Intermediate Client Statement 5
[Frightened] I'm drinking a lot more these days.

Assess and adjust the difficulty before moving to the next difficulty level (see Step 3 in the exercise instructions).

ADVANCED-LEVEL CLIENT STATEMENTS FOR EXERCISE 4
Advanced Client Statement 1
[Frustrated] I sleep about 3 or 4 hours a night.
Advanced Client Statement 2
[Confident] I think I'm ready to start exercising again.
Advanced Client Statement 3
[Unconcerned] I've quit smoking before.
Advanced Client Statement 4
[Annoyed] My partner hates my drinking.
Advanced Client Statement 5
[Thoughtful] I can see how my drinking is really interfering with my life. I know it needs to change.

Assess and adjust the difficulty here (see Step 3 in the exercise instructions). If appropriate, follow the instructions to make the exercise even more challenging (see Appendix A).

Example Clinician Responses: Responding With a Reflection and an Open-Ended Question

Remember: Trainees should attempt to improvise their own responses before reading the example responses. **Do not read the following responses verbatim unless you are having trouble coming up with your own responses!**

EXAMPLE RESPONSES TO BEGINNER-LEVEL CLIENT STATEMENTS FOR EXERCISE 4
Example Response to Beginner Client Statement 1
Your doctor is concerned about your drinking. (Reflection) What are your thoughts about it? (Open-Ended Question)
Example Response to Beginner Client Statement 2
You're ready for a change. (Reflection) What are your thoughts about next steps? (Open-Ended Question)
Example Response to Beginner Client Statement 3
Your friends are encouraging you to get help. (Reflection) What are they worried about? (Open-Ended Question)
Example Response to Beginner Client Statement 4
You'd like to get more sleep at night. (Reflection) How might you do that? (Open-Ended Question)
Example Response to Beginner Client Statement 5
You know you can do this. (Reflection) What's worked for you in the past? (Open-Ended Question) *or* What are your thoughts about next steps? (Open-Ended Question)

EXAMPLE RESPONSES TO INTERMEDIATE-LEVEL CLIENT STATEMENTS FOR EXERCISE 4
Example Response to Intermediate Client Statement 1
Your friends are concerned. (Reflection) What have they said about your cannabis use? What do others think about what's been going on? (Open-Ended Questions)
Example Response to Intermediate Client Statement 2
You're noticing a difference. (Reflection) What differences have you noticed? (Open-Ended Question)
Example Response to Intermediate Client Statement 3
Getting help with the cravings is key for you to quit. (Reflection) What are your thoughts about what might help? (Open-Ended Question)
Example Response to Intermediate Client Statement 4
You're ready to get help. (Reflection) What would you like to be different? (Open-Ended Question)
Example Response to Intermediate Client Statement 5
Your drinking has increased lately. (Reflection) What are your thoughts about your drinking? (Open-Ended Question)

EXAMPLE RESPONSES TO ADVANCED-LEVEL CLIENT STATEMENTS FOR EXERCISE 4
Example Response to Advanced Client Statement 1
You're sleeping 3 to 4 hours a night. (Reflection) What's your nightly sleep goal? (Open-Ended Question)
Example Response to Advanced Client Statement 2
You're thinking about adding exercise back into your life. (Reflection) What would that look like? (Open-Ended Question)
Example Response to Advanced Client Statement 3
You've quit smoking before. (Reflection) What's worked or been helpful when you quit smoking before? (Open-Ended Question)
Example Response to Advanced Client Statement 4
They aren't happy with your drinking. (Reflection) What do they say about your drinking? (Open-Ended Question)
Example Response to Advanced Client Statement 5
You are ready to make a change. (Reflection) What are your thoughts about next steps? How can I help you with your goals to quit drinking? (Open-Ended Questions)

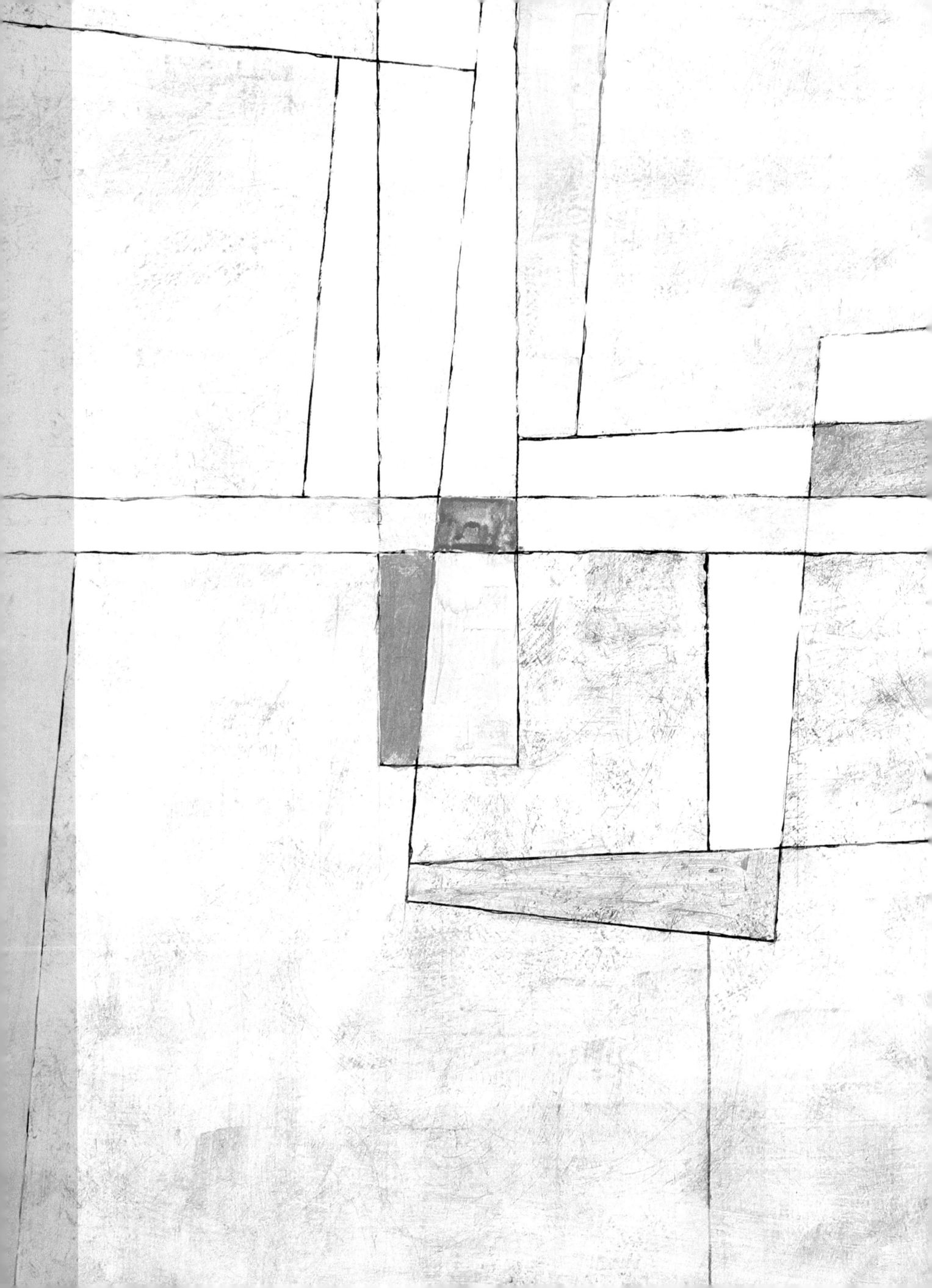

Eliciting Change Talk

Preparations for Exercise 5

1. Read the instructions in Chapter 2.

2. Download the Deliberate Practice Reaction Form and the Deliberate Practice Diary Form at https://www.apa.org/pubs/books/deliberate-practice-motivational-interviewing (see the "Clinician and Practitioner Resources" tab; also available in Appendixes A and B, respectively).

Skill Description

Skill Difficulty Level: Intermediate

Motivational interviewing (MI) has been described as a method that allows the client the opportunity to talk themselves into change. This opportunity is created when the clinician closely attends to client language about a particular change goal or target behavior (e.g., reducing drinking, quitting smoking, exercising more). The clinician intentionally and strategically uses evocative (usually open-ended) questions to elicit change talk from the client (e.g., "What concerns you about your drinking? How will you feel if you exercise more? Why would you like to exercise?").

Change talk includes any client language that expresses reasons why change is needed (e.g., "My hangovers are getting in the way of work"), offers preference for change ("I should cut back on drinking"), moves toward change ("I could stop buying beer on the way home from work"), is an argument for the change ("I would feel better if I drank less"), or expresses confidence that they are able to make the change ("I've cut back before, I can do it again"). Evocative questions are intended to elicit change talk, but there's not a guarantee that the client will answer with change talk. Responses other than change talk may signal that the clinician needs to take a different approach, such as reflecting the client's response or asking a different evocative question that asks for change talk.

https://doi.org/10.1037/0000297-007

To successfully elicit and reinforce change talk, it is helpful for the clinician to identify and differentiate it from sustain talk and neutral talk. *Sustain talk* is language that supports the status quo—to not make a behavior change. Sustain talk is associated with worse treatment outcomes in trials examining the relationship between client language and treatment outcomes, thus MI clinicians often avoid deliberately eliciting client sustain talk ("Why haven't you been able to stop smoking? What keeps you from eating better?") or neutral talk ("How many drinks do you have each day? How old were you when you started smoking pot?"). Following are some example clinician questions that elicit sustain talk.

Examples of Clinician Questions Eliciting Sustain Talk

Sustain Talk Example 1

CLINICIAN: Aren't you worried about the effects of vaping?

CLIENT: I'm not worried about vaping. It's safer than cigarettes.

Sustain Talk Example 2

CLINICIAN: What are your reasons for vaping?

CLIENT: Vaping is healthier for me compared to regular cigarettes.

Sustain Talk Example 3

CLINICIAN: What do you like about drinking?

CLIENT: Drinking is a huge part of my life. I can't imagine what it would be like if I wasn't drinking.

Sustain Talk Example 4

CLINICIAN: Why don't you want to change your drinking?

CLIENT: I'm a good mom. My drinking doesn't interfere with parenting.

Neutral talk includes off-topic material not related to the change goal (e.g., "The traffic was really bad this morning") or factual statements about a change goal or target behavior that do not convey concern, willingness, or need to make a change ("I started drinking when I was 15 years old"). Following are examples of clinician questions that elicit neutral talk.

Examples of Clinician Questions Eliciting Neutral Talk

Neutral Talk Example 1

CLINICIAN: How often are you vaping?

CLIENT: I vape about three or four times a day.

Neutral Talk Example 2

CLINICIAN: How much money have you spent on vaping?

CLIENT: My vaping kit costs about $75.

Neutral Talk Example 3

CLINICIAN: How old were you when you started drinking?

CLIENT: I started drinking when I was in college.

Neutral Talk Example 4

CLINICIAN: Was alcohol a part of your family life growing up?

CLIENT: My mother drank too much when I was a kid.

The types of questions that clinicians can ask clients to elicit change talk instead of sustain talk or neutral talk are outlined in this exercise's skill criteria.

SKILL CRITERIA FOR EXERCISE 5

1. The clinician intentionally and strategically asks an evocative, open-ended question to elicit change talk from the client. This can include the following:

    a. Asking for concerns over a behavior/habit

    b. Asking for the downsides to a behavior/habit

    c. Asking how the client would like things to be different

    d. Asking why the client might want to change

2. The question does not intentionally try to elicit sustain talk or neutral talk.

3. The question does not include the clinician's opinion, advice, or information.

Examples of Clinician Eliciting Change Talk

Change Talk Example 1

CLINICIAN: What concerns do you have about vaping?

CLIENT: I worry about the chemicals in vaping.

Change Talk Example 2

CLINICIAN: What are some of the downsides of vaping?

CLIENT: Vaping costs me a lot of money each month.

Change Talk Example 3

CLINICIAN: How would you like things to be different with your drinking?

CLIENT: I should cut back on my drinking. I've been drinking for a long time, and it's catching up to me.

Change Talk Example 4

CLINICIAN: Why might you want to make a change in your drinking?

CLIENT: I want to be a good mother, not like my mom, who was drunk all the time.

INSTRUCTIONS FOR EXERCISE 5

Step 1: Role-Play and Feedback

- The client says the first beginner client statement. The clinician improvises a response (an evocative, open-ended question) based on the skill criteria.
- The trainer (or, if not available, the client) provides brief feedback based on the skill criteria.
- The client then repeats the same statement, and the clinician again improvises a response. The trainer (or client) again provides brief feedback.

Step 2: Repeat

- Repeat Step 1 for all the statements in the current difficulty level (beginner, intermediate, or advanced).

Step 3: Assess and Adjust Difficulty

- The clinician completes the Deliberate Practice Reaction Form (see Appendix A) and decides whether to make the exercise easier or harder or to repeat the same difficulty level.

Step 4: Repeat for Approximately 15 Minutes

- Repeat Steps 1 to 3 for at least 15 minutes.
- The trainees then switch clinician and client roles and start over.

Now it's your turn! Follow Steps 1 and 2 from the instructions.

Remember: The goal of the role-play is for trainees to practice improvising responses to the client statements (in this case, an evocative, open-ended question that could follow the client statement) in a manner that (a) uses the skill criteria and (b) feels authentic for the trainee. **Example clinician responses for each client statement are provided at the end of this exercise. Trainees should attempt to improvise their own responses before reading the example responses.**

BEGINNER-LEVEL CLIENT STATEMENTS FOR EXERCISE 5
Beginner Client Statement 1
[Matter of fact] I drink about a six-pack of beer a day.
Beginner Client Statement 2
[Sad] My kids really want me to quit smoking.
Beginner Client Statement 3
[Defensive] I like to drink. I got caught drinking on campus and got suspended, but it's not a big deal.
Beginner Client Statement 4
[Concerned] I lose track of time on social media.
Beginner Client Statement 5
[Adamant] I should cut back on my sugar intake.

Assess and adjust the difficulty before moving to the next difficulty level (see Step 3 in the exercise instructions).

INTERMEDIATE-LEVEL CLIENT STATEMENTS FOR EXERCISE 5
Intermediate Client Statement 1
[Frustrated] I've smoked since I was 15 years old. I've never been able to quit.
Intermediate Client Statement 2
[Exasperated] You said I am drinking way more than recommended, but all of my friends drink as much as I do.
Intermediate Client Statement 3
[Frustrated] I used to exercise more regularly. I just don't have time now.
Intermediate Client Statement 4
[Motivated] I should quit smoking. I know it's not good for me.
Intermediate Client Statement 5
[Hopeful] I felt better when I was eating more fruits and vegetables.

Assess and adjust the difficulty before moving to the next difficulty level (see Step 3 in the exercise instructions).

ADVANCED-LEVEL CLIENT STATEMENTS FOR EXERCISE 5
Advanced Client Statement 1
[Contemplative] I think it would be easier for me to exercise if I signed up for an exercise program.
Advanced Client Statement 2
[Slowly, with uncertainty] I've done some stupid things while drunk. And I've had a few blackouts but no legal troubles or anything like that.
Advanced Client Statement 3
[Frustrated] No one understands how hard it is to quit smoking. It's practically impossible.
Advanced Client Statement 4
[Concerned] I know I shouldn't be using my phone while driving.
Advanced Client Statement 5
[Matter of fact] I am not getting enough sleep. I start watching TV and can't pull myself away.

Assess and adjust the difficulty here (see Step 3 in the exercise instructions). If appropriate, follow the instructions to make the exercise even more challenging (see Appendix A).

Example Clinician Responses: Eliciting Change Talk

Remember: Trainees should attempt to improvise their own responses before reading the example responses. **Do not read the following responses verbatim unless you are having trouble coming up with your own responses!**

EXAMPLE RESPONSES TO BEGINNER-LEVEL CLIENT STATEMENTS FOR EXERCISE 5
Example Response to Beginner Client Statement 1
What, if anything, don't you like about your drinking?
Example Response to Beginner Client Statement 2
What do your kids say about your smoking? What are they worried about?
Example Response to Beginner Client Statement 3
What can you do to keep yourself from getting in trouble for drinking on campus again?
Example Response to Beginner Client Statement 4
What else would you like to be doing with that time?
Example Response to Beginner Client Statement 5
What worries you about your sugar intake?

EXAMPLE RESPONSES TO INTERMEDIATE-LEVEL CLIENT STATEMENTS FOR EXERCISE 5
Example Response to Intermediate Client Statement 1
How would things be different if you quit smoking?
Example Response to Intermediate Client Statement 2
What, if any, concerns do you have about hearing that you are drinking more than recommended?
Example Response to Intermediate Client Statement 3
How did you feel when you were exercising regularly?
Example Response to Intermediate Client Statement 4
What worries you about your smoking?
Example Response to Intermediate Client Statement 5
Tell me more about that. How did you feel better when you were eating more fruits and vegetables?

EXAMPLE RESPONSES TO ADVANCED-LEVEL CLIENT STATEMENTS FOR EXERCISE 5
Example Response to Advanced Client Statement 1
What else might help you incorporate exercise into your life?
Example Response to Advanced Client Statement 2
Where do you see yourself in a year or two if you make no changes to your drinking?
Example Response to Advanced Client Statement 3
What would it be like if you were able to quit smoking?
Example Response to Advanced Client Statement 4
What worries you about using your phone while driving?
Example Response to Advanced Client Statement 5
How do you feel when you don't get enough sleep?

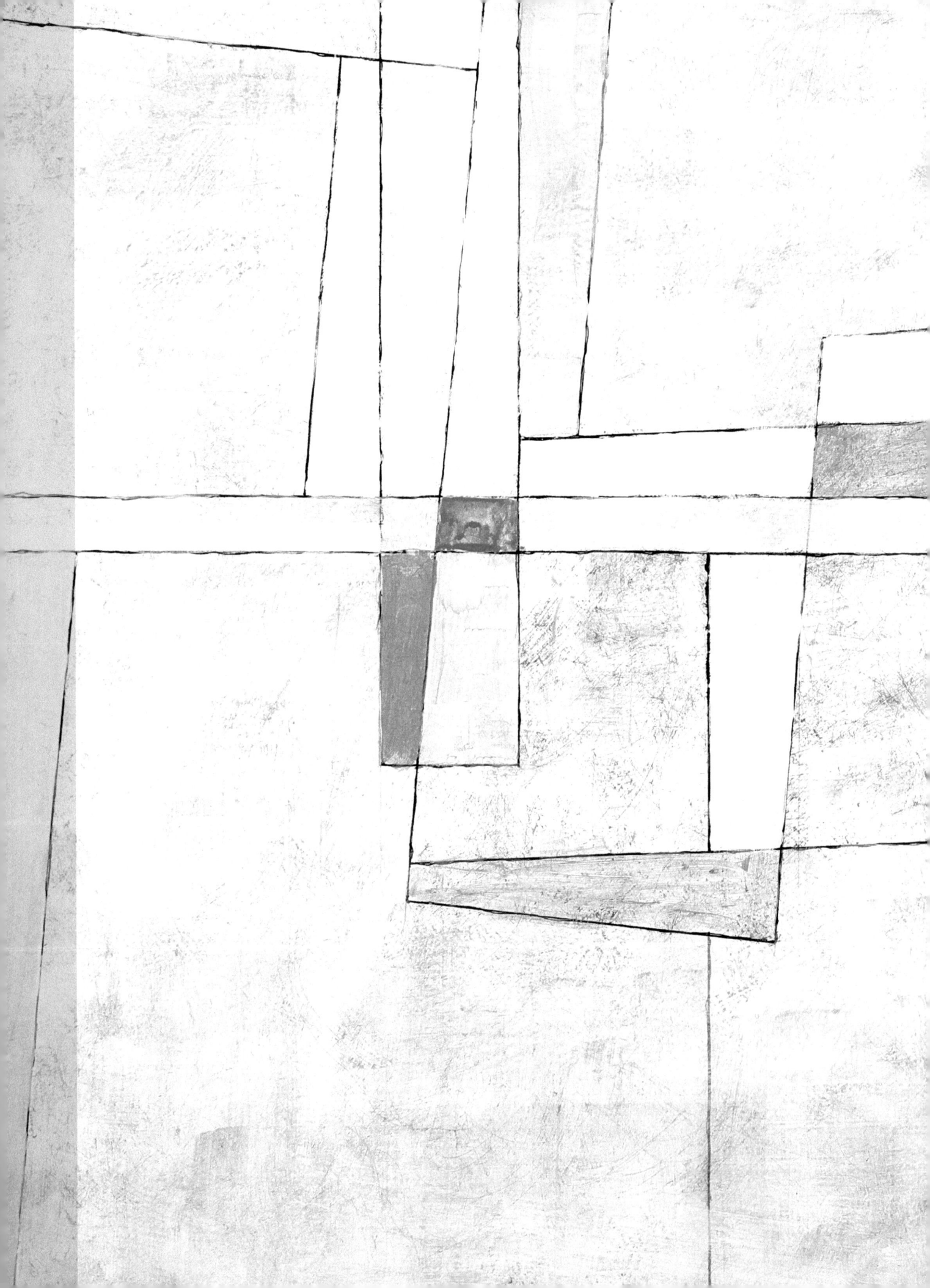

Reflecting Change Talk

Preparations for Exercise 6

1. Read the instructions in Chapter 2.

2. Download the Deliberate Practice Reaction Form and the Deliberate Practice Diary Form at https://www.apa.org/pubs/books/deliberate-practice-motivational-interviewing (see the "Clinician and Practitioner Resources" tab; also available in Appendixes A and B, respectively).

Skill Description

Skill Difficulty Level: Intermediate

In motivational interviewing (MI), clinicians thoughtfully elicit and reinforce a particular type of language, referred to as *client change talk*, which is also covered in Exercise 5. Briefly stated, change talk is client expressions of reasons, preference, movement, arguments for, or confidence toward change. Examples of client change talk include statements such as, "I am spending way too much money on e-cigarettes" and "I feel better when I drink less." As clinicians hear expressions of client change talk, they reinforce, strengthen, and emphasize it with reflections, affirmations, or open-ended questions. In MI, clinicians learn to differentiate client change talk from *client sustain talk*, defined as client expressions of the reasons, preference, movement, arguments, to maintain the status quo or not make a behavior change. Examples of client sustain talk include "Smoking is a way for me to relax and take breaks throughout the day" and "My drinking isn't a problem. I don't need to cut back." Client change talk and sustain talk often occur together in discussions of potential behavior change. This is expected and represents a client's ambivalence about engaging in behavior change. Exercise 7 discusses how to reflect both types of talk in the same statement, but this exercise focuses only on reflecting change talk.

https://doi.org/10.1037/0000297-008

Deliberate Practice in Motivational Interviewing, by J. K. Manuel, D. Ernst, A. Vaz, and T. Rousmaniere

We expect higher levels of client sustain talk in the beginning of MI sessions. MI clinicians may choose to reflect sustain talk as a way of engaging the client in discussions of behavior change. As rapport builds between the client and clinician, which can occur in a matter of minutes, a clinician will begin to shift and focus more exclusively on eliciting and reflecting client change talk. Simple and complex reflections of client change talk, even when the change talk occurs in the presence of sustain talk, are ways to highlight a client's consideration and movement toward change. Simple reflections repeat or rephrase a client's statement. Complex reflections go beyond what a client has stated. Complex reflections add further meaning, emphasis, or emotion to a client statement, based on clinician inference and observation.

SKILL CRITERIA FOR EXERCISE 6

1. The clinician replies to the client with either a *simple reflection* or a *complex reflection*.

   a. A *simple reflection* repeats or rephrases a client's statement.

   b. A *complex reflection* goes beyond the client statements to add further meaning, emphasis, or emotion.

2. The reflection only reinforces the Change Talk in the client's words and does not reinforce the client's sustain talk. (See Exercise 5 for a definition of sustain talk.)

Examples of Clinician Reflecting Change Talk

Example 1

CLIENT: [*concerned*] I should stop drinking soda. I know it's not good for me.

CLINICIAN: You should stop drinking soda. (Simple Reflection)

or

CLINICIAN: You are worried about how soda may be affecting you. (Complex Reflection)

Example 2

CLIENT: [*frustrated*] I've thought about talking to someone about my depression. I wish I felt better. I just don't even know where to start.

CLINICIAN: You've thought about talking to someone about your depression. (Simple Reflection)

or

CLINICIAN: You've been considering this for a while. You're tired of feeling this way. (Complex Reflection)

Example 3

CLIENT: [*annoyed*] I am spending too much on takeout food. I need to start cooking at home. It's just so hard to plan ahead and find the time to cook.

CLINICIAN: You're spending a lot of money on takeout. (Simple Reflection)

or

CLINICIAN: You are tired of spending so much money on takeout. You have other things to do with your money. (Complex Reflection)

INSTRUCTIONS FOR EXERCISE 6

Step 1: Role-Play and Feedback

- The client says the first beginner client statement. The clinician improvises a response based on the skill criteria.
- The trainer (or, if not available, the client) provides brief feedback based on the skill criteria.
- The client then repeats the same statement, and the clinician again improvises a response. The trainer (or client) again provides brief feedback.

Step 2: Repeat

- Repeat Step 1 for all the statements in the current difficulty level (beginner, intermediate, or advanced).

Step 3: Assess and Adjust Difficulty

- The clinician completes the Deliberate Practice Reaction Form (see Appendix A) and decides whether to make the exercise easier or harder or to repeat the same difficulty level.

Step 4: Repeat for Approximately 15 Minutes

- Repeat Steps 1 to 3 for at least 15 minutes.
- The trainees then switch clinician and client roles and start over.

> **Now it's your turn! Follow Steps 1 and 2 from the instructions.**

Remember: The goal of the role-play is for trainees to practice improvising responses to the client statements in a manner that (a) uses the skill criteria and (b) feels authentic for the trainee. **Example clinician responses for each client statement are provided at the end of this exercise. Trainees should attempt to improvise their own responses before reading the example responses.**

BEGINNER-LEVEL CLIENT STATEMENTS FOR EXERCISE 6
Beginner Client Statement 1
[Concerned] I'm worried about my eating. I love sugar and carbs and that's all I've been eating. I've gained weight and feel terrible.
Beginner Client Statement 2
[Surprised] My doctor asked me about my drinking and said I drink more than the recommended amount. That really surprised me and worried me a little. But my friends drink as much as I do, so I can't see why it's a problem. It seems normal to me.
Beginner Client Statement 3
[Apprehensive] The blackouts scare me. I know I should do something about my drinking. I really like drinking though. I'd hate to give it up entirely.
Beginner Client Statement 4
[Matter of fact] Pot helps me to sleep at night. I might be using it too much. It's legal, though, so how bad can it be?
Beginner Client Statement 5
[Adamant] I am spending way too much money on cigarettes. I just can't quit.

🛑 **Assess and adjust the difficulty before moving to the next difficulty level (see Step 3 in the exercise instructions).**

INTERMEDIATE-LEVEL CLIENT STATEMENTS FOR EXERCISE 6
Intermediate Client Statement 1
[Uncertain] I know I drink too much. I think I should cut back, but it's how I relax at night.
Intermediate Client Statement 2
[Exasperated] I keep saying I am not going to look at my phone while I drive, but it happens without me even realizing it.
Intermediate Client Statement 3
[Irritated] I always get sick from the flu shot. I don't want to get the flu, but I don't want to get sick from the flu shot either.
Intermediate Client Statement 4
[Concerned] I think caffeine is starting to mess up my sleep. I drink it to stay awake throughout the day, but then I can't sleep at night and I know I function better with a full night of sleep.
Intermediate Client Statement 5
[Frustrated] I spend all day on social media. I tell myself I will only check it for a few minutes and then over an hour has gone by. It's how I stay in touch with my friends.

Assess and adjust the difficulty before moving to the next difficulty level (see Step 3 in the exercise instructions).

ADVANCED-LEVEL CLIENT STATEMENTS FOR EXERCISE 6
Advanced Client Statement 1
[Hostile] Should I quit smoking? Sure. Can I quit smoking? No. I've tried before, and it's never worked.
Advanced Client Statement 2
[Adamant] Oxy is the only thing that helps with the pain since I hurt my back. The doctors are telling me it's too dangerous to keep using it. They just think I'm addicted. You probably do too. No one believes me. I'm in pain!
Advanced Client Statement 3
[Irritated] All of my friends drink as much as I do. I don't want to get a DUI again, but my drinking isn't a big problem. You're probably going to tell me to quit, but I don't need to.
Advanced Client Statement 4
[Hesitant] I don't like using condoms, but they give me some reassurance.
Advanced Client Statement 5
[Hostile] Of course you want to talk about my smoking. You are going to tell me to quit, like everyone else. If it was that easy, I would. I don't want to be a smoker.

> ✋ **Assess and adjust the difficulty here (see Step 3 in the exercise instructions). If appropriate, follow the instructions to make the exercise even more challenging (see Appendix A).**

Example Clinician Responses: Reflecting Change Talk

Remember: Trainees should attempt to improvise their own responses before reading the example responses. **Do not read the following responses verbatim unless you are having trouble coming up with your own responses!**

EXAMPLE RESPONSES TO BEGINNER-LEVEL CLIENT STATEMENTS FOR EXERCISE 6
Example Response to Beginner Client Statement 1
You are worried about your eating. (Simple Reflection) or You are ready for a change and you want to feel better. (Complex Reflection)
Example Response to Beginner Client Statement 2
Your doctor indicated that you're drinking more than the recommended amount and that worried you. (Simple Reflection) or This is a lot for you to take in. This news, that you're drinking more than is recommended, has you thinking about your drinking in a different way. (Complex Reflection)
Example Response to Beginner Client Statement 3
The blackouts scare you. (Simple Reflection) or The blackouts were a warning sign for you. You worry about what might happen if you don't make any changes to your drinking. (Complex Reflection)
Example Response to Beginner Client Statement 4
You think you might be using too much pot. (Simple Reflection) or Your pot use worries you. (Complex Reflection)
Example Response to Beginner Client Statement 5
You're spending too much money on cigarettes. (Simple Reflection) or You're frustrated with how much money you are spending on cigarettes and you want to make a change. (Complex Reflection)

EXAMPLE RESPONSES TO INTERMEDIATE-LEVEL CLIENT STATEMENTS FOR EXERCISE 6
Example Response to Intermediate Client Statement 1
You know you drink too much. (Simple Reflection) *or* Your drinking worries you and you want to make a change. (Complex Reflection)
Example Response to Intermediate Client Statement 2
You keep trying to not look at your phone while driving. (Simple Reflection) *or* It scares you to use your phone while you drive. (Complex Reflection)
Example Response to Intermediate Client Statement 3
You don't want to get the flu. (Simple Reflection) *or* Your health is important to you. (Complex Reflection)
Example Response to Intermediate Client Statement 4
Caffeine is really getting in the way of your sleep. (Simple Reflection) *or* You're really thinking that too much caffeine might be causing you some problems. (Complex Reflection)
Example Response to Intermediate Client Statement 5
You spend a lot of time on social media. (Simple Reflection) *or* You really want to cut back on your social media use. (Complex Reflection)

EXAMPLE RESPONSES TO ADVANCED-LEVEL CLIENT STATEMENTS FOR EXERCISE 6
Example Response to Advanced Client Statement 1
You've tried to quit smoking before and think you should quit smoking again. (Simple Reflection) or You've been trying to quit smoking for a long time and you want to kick this habit. (Complex Reflection)
Example Response to Advanced Client Statement 2
The doctors have told you that it's too dangerous to keep using oxy. (Simple Reflection) or You'd really like to find a way to manage the pain without oxy. (Complex Reflection)
Example Response to Advanced Client Statement 3
You don't want to get a DUI again. (Simple Reflection) or Staying out of trouble and avoiding another DUI is a big priority for you. (Complex Reflection)
Example Response to Advanced Client Statement 4
Condoms give you some reassurance. (Simple Reflection) or Using condoms gives you peace of mind. There's a sense of safety with them. (Complex Reflection)
Example Response to Advanced Client Statement 5
You don't want to be a smoker. (Simple Reflection) or A lot of people are worried about you and are telling you to quit smoking. (Complex Reflection)

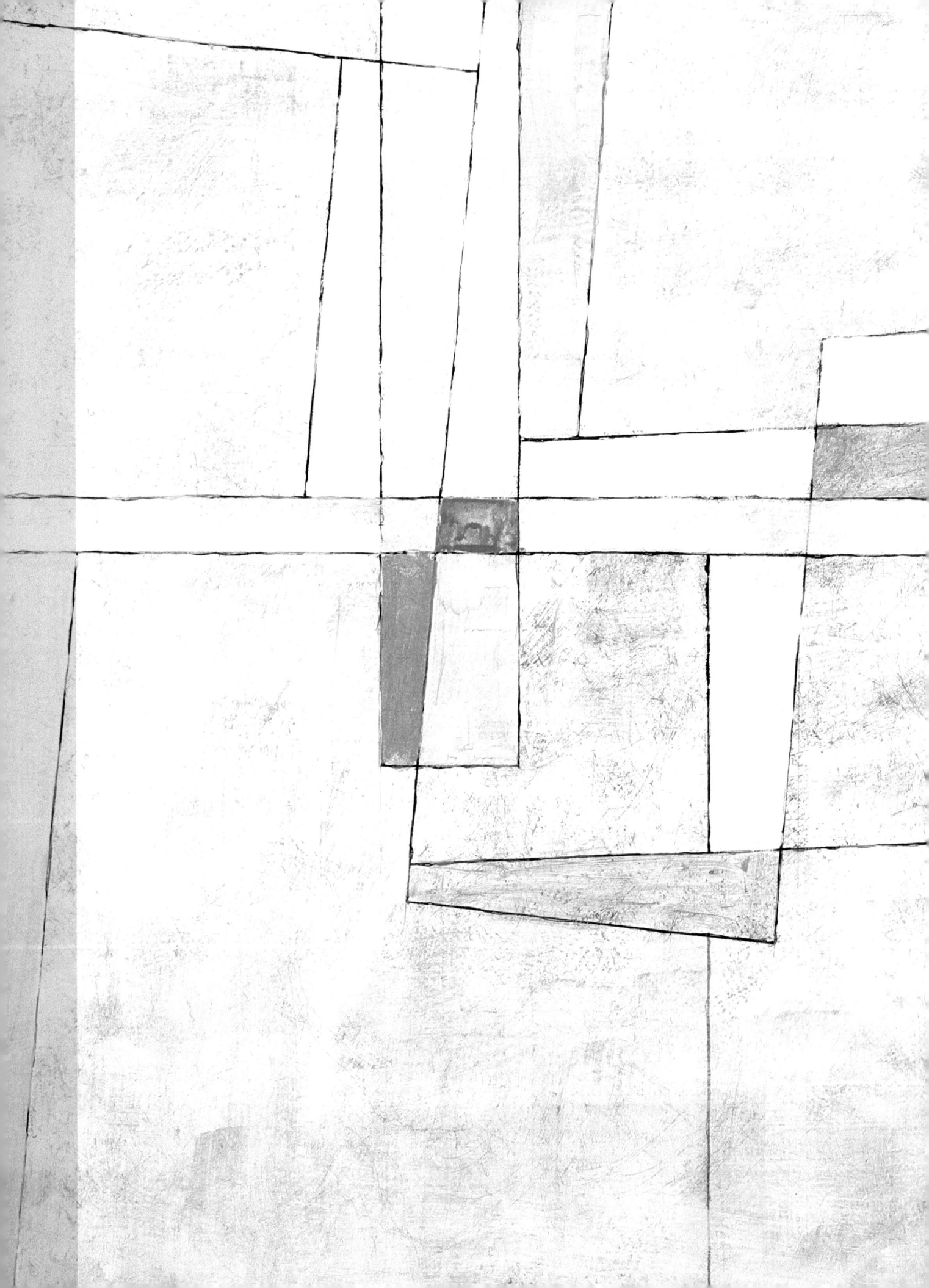

Double-Sided Reflections

Preparations for Exercise 7

1. Read the instructions in Chapter 2.

2. Download the Deliberate Practice Reaction Form and the Deliberate Practice Diary Form at https://www.apa.org/pubs/books/deliberate-practice-motivational-interviewing (see the "Clinician and Practitioner Resources" tab; also available in Appendixes A and B, respectively).

Skill Description

Skill Difficulty Level: Intermediate

This exercise helps trainees practice double-sided reflections, a particular type of reflection. Motivational interviewing (MI) is based on the assumption that ambivalence is normal and expected in discussions of behavior change. When clients are ambivalent about making a behavior change, they will naturally offer both change talk and sustain talk, as described in Exercise 6. *Client change talk* includes reasons, preference, movement, arguments, or confidence for change. Conversely, *client sustain talk* includes expressions of reasons, preference, movement, or arguments to maintain the status quo or not engage in a behavior change.

MI clinicians will selectively attend to sustain talk, giving preference to client change talk. This practice is based on both MI theory and the results of prior research studies of MI that have shown that the more sustain talk occurs and is reinforced in a session, the less likely a client is to make a behavior change. However, clinicians do not want to entirely ignore client sustain talk because doing so may lead clients to feel misunderstood and pushed toward behavior change. A common method of attending to client expressions of both change talk and sustain talk while giving preference to change talk is called a *double-sided reflection*. Here, the clinician first reflects sustain talk,

https://doi.org/10.1037/0000297-009

then follows that with an "and" statement that reflects change talk. The order of the change talk and sustain talk is important because clients will often follow the clinician's last statement. Thus, if a clinician ends with sustain talk, the client will likely continue to elaborate on their sustain talk. Additionally, it's important to link the change talk and sustain talk with the word "and" because the clinician is reflecting two things that are simultaneously true for the client. For example, a client may be "unsure how I will socialize with friends if I'm not drinking" and "be spending too much money on alcohol." A "but" statement linking change talk and sustain talk discounts or limits the first part of the statement in a way that can cause a client to feel defensive or misunderstood. A double-sided reflection that reflects sustain talk and change talk highlights the client's ambivalence while encouraging further change talk by ending with a reflection of client change talk.

SKILL CRITERIA FOR EXERCISE 7

1. The clinician replies to the client with a double-sided reflection by first reflecting the sustain talk, followed by a reflection of client change talk.
2. The sustain talk and change talk are linked with the word "and."
3. Avoid using the word "but."

Examples of Clinicians Using Double-Sided Reflections

Example 1

CLIENT: [*concerned*] I should stop drinking soda. I know it's not good for me, but I love having a soda in the afternoon. It's a little treat in my day.

CLINICIAN: Your afternoon soda is a treat for you, and you're worried about how it may be affecting you.

Example 2

CLIENT: [*frustrated*] I've thought about talking to someone about my depression. I wish I felt better. I just don't even know where to start. How do you even find a therapist?

CLINICIAN: It's overwhelming, and you are ready to start feeling better.

Example 3

CLIENT: [*matter of fact*] I am spending too much on takeout food. I need to start cooking at home. It's just so hard to plan ahead and find the time to cook.

CLINICIAN: You don't have a lot of time for cooking, and you're ready to figure out how to cook at home.

INSTRUCTIONS FOR EXERCISE 7

Step 1: Role-Play and Feedback

- The client says the first beginner client statement. The clinician improvises a response based on the skill criteria.
- The trainer (or, if not available, the client) provides brief feedback based on the skill criteria.
- The client then repeats the same statement, and the clinician again improvises a response. The trainer (or client) again provides brief feedback.

Step 2: Repeat

- Repeat Step 1 for all the statements in the current difficulty level (beginner, intermediate, or advanced).

Step 3: Assess and Adjust Difficulty

- The clinician completes the Deliberate Practice Reaction Form (see Appendix A) and decides whether to make the exercise easier or harder or to repeat the same difficulty level.

Step 4: Repeat for Approximately 15 Minutes

- Repeat Steps 1 to 3 for at least 15 minutes.
- The trainees then switch clinician and client roles and start over.

Now it's your turn! Follow Steps 1 and 2 from the instructions.

Remember: The goal of the role-play is for trainees to practice improvising responses to the client statements in a manner that (a) uses the skill criteria and (b) feels authentic for the trainee. **Example clinician responses for each client statement are provided at the end of this exercise. Trainees should attempt to improvise their own responses before reading the example responses.**

BEGINNER-LEVEL CLIENT STATEMENTS FOR EXERCISE 7
Beginner Client Statement 1
[Concerned] I need to eat better and cut back on the sugary drinks. That will require me to plan meals and snacks, which is hard because I'm so busy. I know I need to do something though. I've gained weight and have noticed a huge difference in how I feel.
Beginner Client Statement 2
[Thoughtful] My primary care provider told me I should be careful about how much cannabis I am using. She said it could be causing my sleep problems. It's how I unwind though. I look forward to it at the end of the day.
Beginner Client Statement 3
[Frustrated] I got a DUI a few years ago. That scared me. I don't want to have any more legal problems, and I know I've started to head in that territory. I need to make some changes but I'd hate to give up drinking entirely.
Beginner Client Statement 4
[Frustrated] I want to quit smoking. I hate how much I spend on cigarettes. I've tried too many times and not been successful.
Beginner Client Statement 5
[Matter of fact] I love having a martini, or two or three, after work. My friends and I go to happy hour and unwind. We work hard and deserve the break. Sure, the blackouts scared me, but I won't let that happen again.

Assess and adjust the difficulty before moving to the next difficulty level (see Step 3 in the exercise instructions).

INTERMEDIATE-LEVEL CLIENT STATEMENTS FOR EXERCISE 7
Intermediate Client Statement 1
[Sad] I know I shouldn't text and drive. It's so hard to resist. Sometimes I do it without even thinking about it.
Intermediate Client Statement 2
[Concerned] I don't want to get the flu shot. I always feel sick when I get it. I know that's stupid, and I am taking a bigger risk by skipping it.
Intermediate Client Statement 3
[Frustrated] I am drinking way too much caffeine, and it's starting to mess up my sleep. I drink it to stay awake throughout the day, but then I can't sleep at night, and I know I function better with a full night of sleep.
Intermediate Client Statement 4
[Exasperated] I get sucked into video games all of the time. They're fun. My grades are getting worse. I keep telling myself I will stop playing but then I do it again.
Intermediate Client Statement 5
[Adamant] I am going to start exercising more. I have a plan, I have the equipment, I'm all set. I've said this probably 500 times and never been successful so it's hard to believe that this will work but I will try.

Assess and adjust the difficulty before moving to the next difficulty level (see Step 3 in the exercise instructions).

ADVANCED-LEVEL CLIENT STATEMENTS FOR EXERCISE 7
Advanced Client Statement 1
[Defensive] I'm really tired of hearing about my smoking. Have you ever smoked? It's not easy to quit. I know I should quit but no one seems to understand how hard it is to quit.
Advanced Client Statement 2
[Frustrated] I'm not sure why I'm even here. Everyone tells me I am depressed and need help. It's not like you can wave a magic wand and make me feel better.
Advanced Client Statement 3
[Concerned] I've gone to residential treatment programs before. They don't help. They may work for some people but not me. What do you think I should do?
Advanced Client Statement 4
[Sad] I'm not sure anyone understands how much I am suffering with this back pain. I want to feel better, but everyone is focused on my meds and not how I feel.
Advanced Client Statement 5
[Exasperated] I think it's ridiculous that I failed a drug test for smoking weed. Now I could get fired and have to come here and talk to you.

🛑 **Assess and adjust the difficulty here (see Step 3 in the exercise instructions). If appropriate, follow the instructions to make the exercise even more challenging (see Appendix A).**

Example Clinician Responses: Double-Sided Reflections

Remember: Trainees should attempt to improvise their own responses before reading the example responses. **Do not read the following responses verbatim unless you are having trouble coming up with your own responses!**

EXAMPLE RESPONSES TO BEGINNER-LEVEL CLIENT STATEMENTS FOR EXERCISE 7
Example Response to Beginner Client Statement 1
Eating better requires some tough changes and you're ready. You want to eat healthier, lose some weight, and feel better.
Example Response to Beginner Client Statement 2
You've been using cannabis to unwind at the end of the day, and you worry that it may be interfering with your sleep.
Example Response to Beginner Client Statement 3
You're not ready to quit drinking entirely, and you want to make some changes so you don't have any more legal problems.
Example Response to Beginner Client Statement 4
It's been tough to quit smoking, and you're willing to give it another try.
Example Response to Beginner Client Statement 5
Drinking is a way for you to relax with your friends, and the blackouts scared you.

EXAMPLE RESPONSES TO INTERMEDIATE-LEVEL CLIENT STATEMENTS FOR EXERCISE 7
Example Response to Intermediate Client Statement 1
It's almost a reaction to answer a text while you drive, and you really worry what might happen if you keep doing it.
Example Response to Intermediate Client Statement 2
You're tempted to skip the flu shot, and, deep down, you know you're safer if you get it.
Example Response to Intermediate Client Statement 3
Caffeine helps you stay alert throughout the day, and it's really messing up your sleep.
Example Response to Intermediate Client Statement 4
Video games have been fun for you, and they're not worth interfering with your grades.
Example Response to Intermediate Client Statement 5
It's been hard to get into an exercise routine, and you're ready now.

EXAMPLE RESPONSES TO ADVANCED-LEVEL CLIENT STATEMENTS FOR EXERCISE 7
Example Response to Advanced Client Statement 1
You're really frustrated. Quitting smoking has been challenging and you're wanting more support so that you can successfully quit.
Example Response to Advanced Client Statement 2
You're not sure if or how I can help you, and you're here because you do want to feel better.
Example Response to Advanced Client Statement 3
You're not sure that a residential treatment program is the right choice for you, and you want to find a program that really meets your needs.
Example Response to Advanced Client Statement 4
Your back pain has caused you a lot of suffering, and you really want to feel better.
Example Response to Advanced Client Statement 5
This whole situation is frustrating, and at the same time, this job is really important to you and you don't want to lose it.

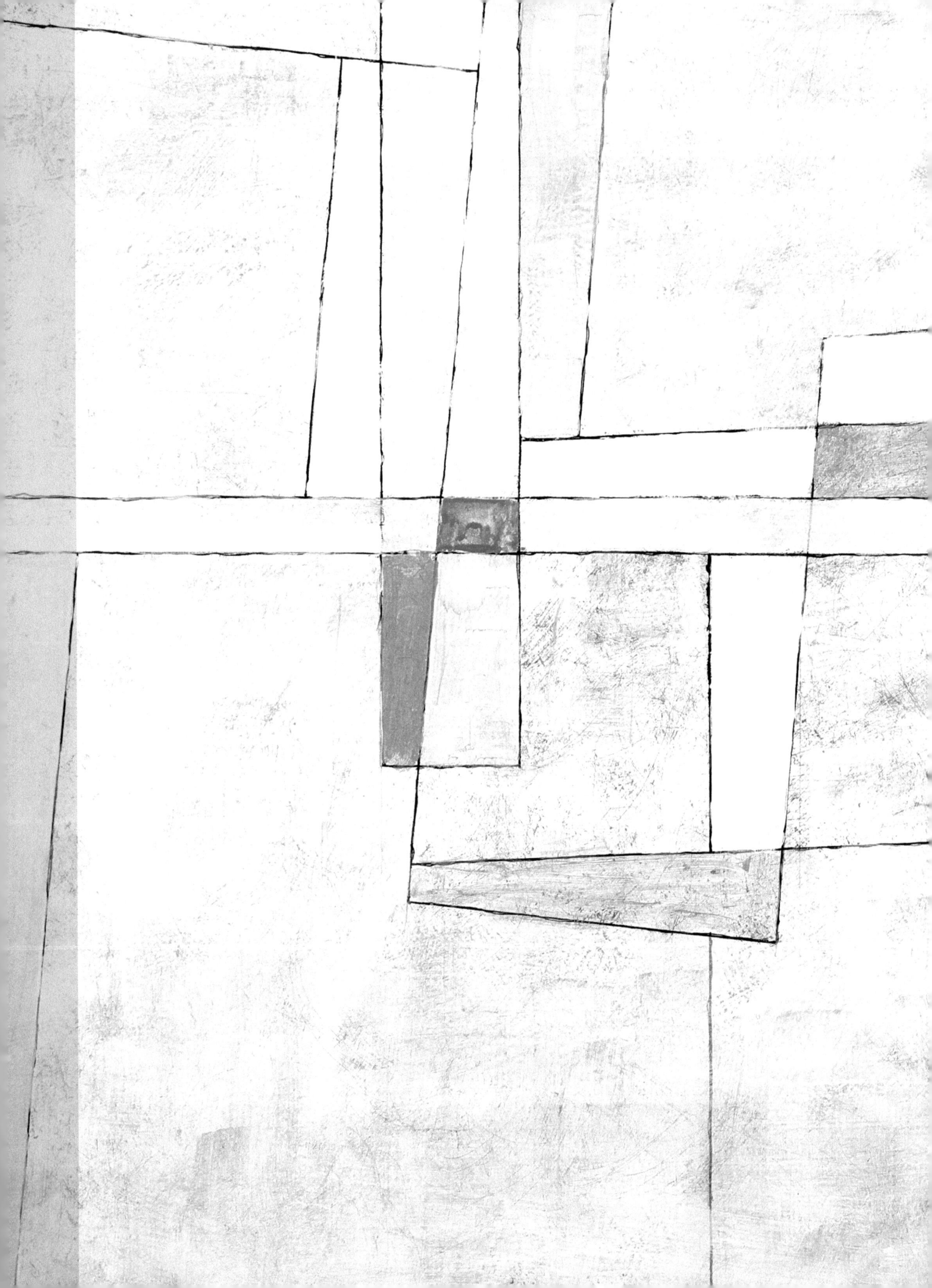

Dancing With Discord

Preparations for Exercise 8

1. Read the instructions in Chapter 2.

2. Download the Deliberate Practice Reaction Form and the Deliberate Practice Diary Form at https://www.apa.org/pubs/books/deliberate-practice-motivational-interviewing (see the "Clinician and Practitioner Resources" tab; also available in Appendixes A and B, respectively).

Skill Description

Skill Difficulty Level: Intermediate

When a clinician is successfully using motivational interviewing (MI) skills, it can appear as if the client and clinician are "dancing" together. That is, they are engaged in a collaborative, back-and-forth discussion where both participants are engaged and moving forward together toward a shared goal. At times, this dance can shift into "wrestling," which can be the result of the clinician's behavior (e.g., perhaps the clinician gets ahead of the client or becomes prescriptive), or it can be due to a client's underlying ambivalence about behavior change. In MI, this shift is referred to as *discord*. Discord resembles sustain talk language in that it often moves away from a targeted behavior change. Additionally, discord differs from sustain talk in that it represents a conflict or a tension between the client and clinician ("You can't understand how hard it is to quit drinking"), whereas sustain talk represents conflict or tension toward a targeted behavior ("It is impossible to quit drinking"). Discord can serve as a warning sign to clinicians that they want to proceed carefully and may even need to change their approach. The best way to proceed is to embrace ("dance with") the client's discord using a simple or complex reflection. Reflections of discord express empathy to the client and highlight the collaborative nature of MI. The goal of "dancing with discord" is to engage the client so that a collaborative discussion regarding a particular behavior change can occur or continue.

https://doi.org/10.1037/0000297-010

Deliberate Practice in Motivational Interviewing, by J. K. Manuel, D. Ernst, A. Vaz, and T. Rousmaniere

SKILL CRITERIA FOR EXERCISE 8

1. The clinician responds to the client with a *simple reflection* or a *complex reflection*.
   a. A *simple reflection* repeats or rephrases the client statement.
   b. A *complex reflection* goes beyond the client statements to add further meaning, emphasis or emotion.
2. The clinician avoids arguing, confronting, or shaming the client with their response.
3. The clinician avoids educating, informing, or persuading the client with their response.

Examples of Clinicians Dancing With Discord

Example 1

CLIENT: [*exasperated*] You're the third person today to ask me about my smoking. Yes, I smoke. No, you can't get me to quit.

CLINICIAN: A few people have asked you about your smoking today. (Simple Reflection)

or

CLINICIAN: You're tired of being asked about your smoking. (Complex Reflection)

Example 2

CLIENT: [*annoyed*] I'm late to meet with you because there's no parking around here. Why do you have to make it so difficult for people to get help?

CLINICIAN: The parking situation has been difficult. (Simple Reflection)

or

CLINICIAN: Parking was a challenge today. You persevered because it's important for you to get help. (Complex Reflection)

INSTRUCTIONS FOR EXERCISE 8

Step 1: Role-Play and Feedback

- The client says the first beginner client statement. The clinician improvises a response based on the skill criteria.
- The trainer (or, if not available, the client) provides brief feedback based on the skill criteria.
- The client then repeats the same statement, and the clinician again improvises a response. The trainer (or client) again provides brief feedback.

Step 2: Repeat

- Repeat Step 1 for all the statements in the current difficulty level (beginner, intermediate, or advanced).

Step 3: Assess and Adjust Difficulty

- The clinician completes the Deliberate Practice Reaction Form (see Appendix A) and decides whether to make the exercise easier or harder or to repeat the same difficulty level.

Step 4: Repeat for Approximately 15 Minutes

- Repeat Steps 1 to 3 for at least 15 minutes.
- The trainees then switch clinician and client roles and start over.

Now it's your turn! Follow Steps 1 and 2 from the instructions.

Remember: The goal of the role-play is for trainees to practice improvising responses to the client statements in a manner that (a) uses the skill criteria and (b) feels authentic for the trainee. **Example clinician responses for each client statement are provided at the end of this exercise. Trainees should attempt to improvise their own responses before reading the example responses.**

BEGINNER-LEVEL CLIENT STATEMENTS FOR EXERCISE 8
Beginner Client Statement 1
[Matter of fact] My doctor thinks you can help me, but I don't see how that's possible.
Beginner Client Statement 2
[Annoyed] That intake form was really long and took forever. I came here to get help, not to fill out lots of paperwork for you.
Beginner Client Statement 3
[Frustrated] How long is this appointment going to take? I'm busy and don't have all day to talk to you.
Beginner Client Statement 4
[Defensive] Are you here to tell me to quit smoking?
Beginner Client Statement 5
[Sad] No one here understands what I'm going through. You just keep passing me off to another provider.

Assess and adjust the difficulty before moving to the next difficulty level (see Step 3 in the exercise instructions).

INTERMEDIATE-LEVEL CLIENT STATEMENTS FOR EXERCISE 8
Intermediate Client Statement 1
[Matter of fact] Have you ever smoked? If not, you can't help me.
Intermediate Client Statement 2
[Annoyed] You ask a lot of questions.
Intermediate Client Statement 3
[Exasperated] You think you can help me with my PTSD? How old are you anyway?
Intermediate Client Statement 4
[Frustrated] I don't think you're listening to me.
Intermediate Client Statement 5
[Sad] You don't understand what I'm going through.

🤚 **Assess and adjust the difficulty before moving to the next difficulty level (see Step 3 in the exercise instructions).**

ADVANCED-LEVEL CLIENT STATEMENTS FOR EXERCISE 8
Advanced Client Statement 1
[Frustrated] You might have gone to a lot of school, but you have no idea what this is really like.
Advanced Client Statement 2
[Adamant] Have you ever used cannabis? I don't think you can understand how it's helpful if you've never tried it.
Advanced Client Statement 3
[Annoyed] All you want to do is talk about my drinking. I'm tired of talking about it.
Advanced Client Statement 4
[Defensive] I disagree with you. I think you're totally wrong.
Advanced Client Statement 5
[Adamant] What you're saying is totally ridiculous.

🤚 **Assess and adjust the difficulty here (see Step 3 in the exercise instructions). If appropriate, follow the instructions to make the exercise even more challenging (see Appendix A).**

Example Clinician Responses: Dancing With Discord

Remember: Trainees should attempt to improvise their own responses before reading the example responses. **Do not read the following responses verbatim unless you are having trouble coming up with your own responses!**

EXAMPLE RESPONSES TO BEGINNER-LEVEL CLIENT STATEMENTS FOR EXERCISE 8
Example Response to Beginner Client Statement 1
You're not sure I can help you.
Example Response to Beginner Client Statement 2
The intake process was frustrating. You came here ready to get started.
Example Response to Beginner Client Statement 3
You're pretty busy and not so happy about being here today.
Example Response to Beginner Client Statement 4
You have your own thoughts about smoking and don't want anyone to tell you what to do.
Example Response to Beginner Client Statement 5
This has been frustrating. You really want to be heard.

EXAMPLE RESPONSES TO INTERMEDIATE-LEVEL CLIENT STATEMENTS FOR EXERCISE 8
Example Response to Intermediate Client Statement 1
You really want to be understood.
Example Response to Intermediate Client Statement 2
This is frustrating.
Example Response to Intermediate Client Statement 3
You're wondering if I can help you.
Example Response to Intermediate Client Statement 4
You don't feel heard right now.
Example Response to Intermediate Client Statement 5
You want me to understand what's going on for you.

EXAMPLE RESPONSES TO ADVANCED-LEVEL CLIENT STATEMENTS FOR EXERCISE 8
Example Response to Advanced Client Statement 1
This has been really hard for you.
Example Response to Advanced Client Statement 2
Cannabis has been helping you, and you're not sure I understand that piece.
Example Response to Advanced Client Statement 3
This has been frustrating. You have other goals for our time together.
Example Response to Advanced Client Statement 4
You see this differently.
Example Response to Advanced Client Statement 5
This doesn't match up for you.

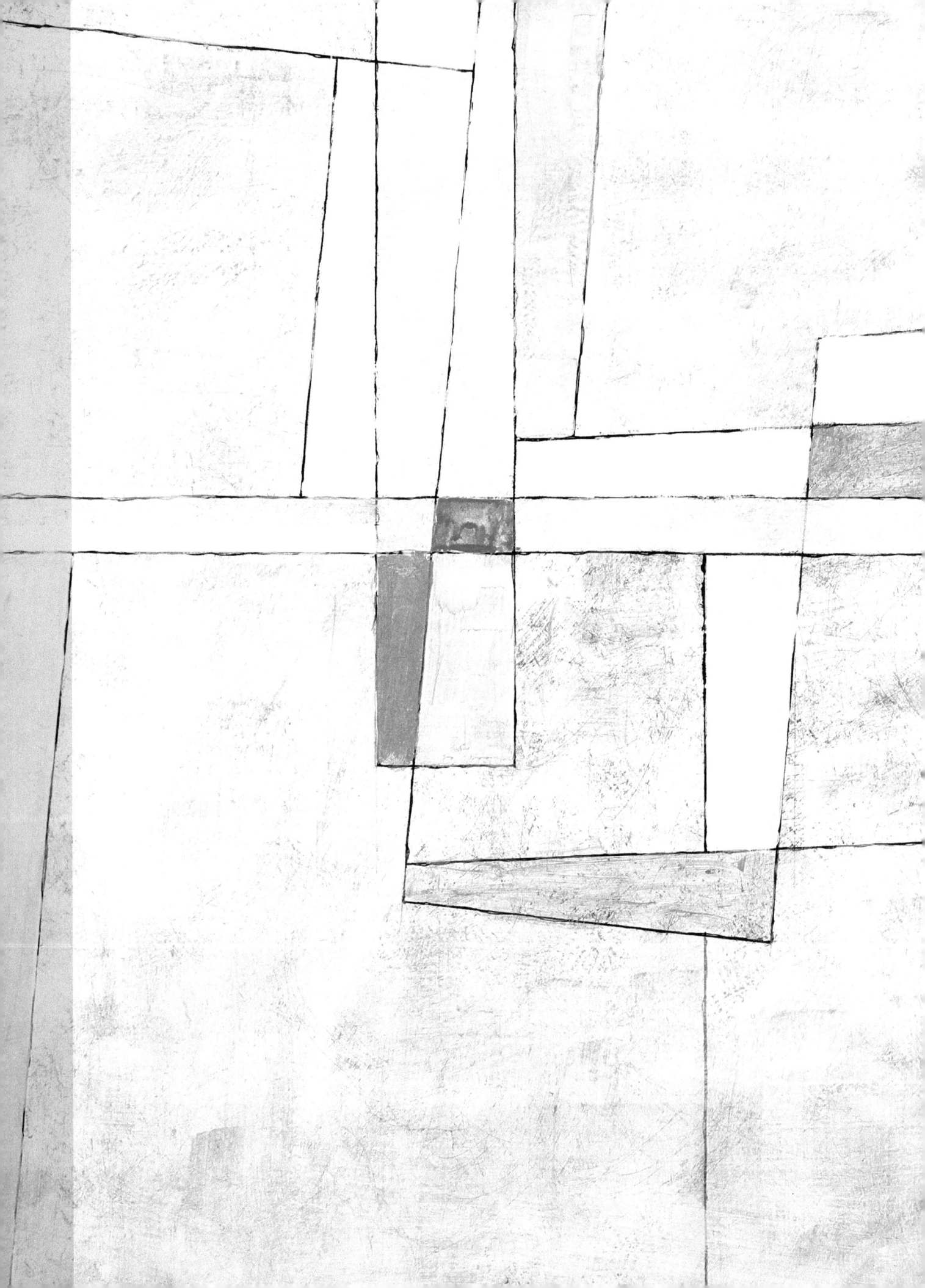

Simple and Complex Affirmations

Preparations for Exercise 9

1. Read the instructions in Chapter 2.

2. Download the Deliberate Practice Reaction Form and the Deliberate Practice Diary Form at https://www.apa.org/pubs/books/deliberate-practice-motivational-interviewing (see the "Clinician and Practitioner Resources" tab; also available in Appendixes A and B, respectively).

Skill Description

Skill Difficulty Level: Advanced

Client affirmations are a core skill in motivational interviewing (MI). Affirmations are a way for the clinician to express unconditional positive regard, an essential condition for change in MI. Affirming involves valuing, noting, or appreciating a client's strengths, efforts, accomplishments, characteristics, and/or virtues. The clinician is encouraged to listen to the client through a strengths-based lens, deemphasizing what is seen as weakness or pathology, in favor of expressing optimism and hope and trusting the client's inner drive toward health and well-being. To be effective, affirmations must be specific, genuine, and not overused (as this can detract or seem superficial). Affirmations may be classified as simple or complex, and both are useful, although the most powerful affirmations are often complex reflections.

Simple affirmations are like the frosting on a cake: not enough and the cake is dry, too much and the cake is sickeningly sweet and inedible. This is to say, simple affirmations should be used sparingly and intentionally. Simple affirmations are statements that express

- Appreciation (e.g., "I really appreciate your coming in today. I know it was not easy to get here.")
- Encouragement (e.g., "You can do this! You've got what it takes.")
- Reinforcement of client effort (e.g., "Good job on the homework, keep it up!")

https://doi.org/10.1037/0000297-011

Complex affirmations are typically also complex reflections in that they are focused on the deeper meaning of the client's strengths or abilities. They require listening for those strengths, often in the midst of a chaotic conversation about the client's problems. Strong affirmations are consistent with the mechanisms of change in MI and highlight movement toward a behavioral change, efficacy, confidence, choice, a prized characteristic, an effort made, or a client's success. These affirmations must be genuine and intentional. A meaningful complex affirmation is worth several simple affirmations. Typically, in a conversation, there may be one or two complex affirmations. Here are some examples of complex affirmations:

- "You have shown such perseverance in face of your difficulties. Even when things get tough, you hang in there."

- "Being a person of your word is really important to you. You have followed through even when it cost you a lot."

Simple affirmations are generally easier than complex affirmations, so we have split them up accordingly in this exercise. The beginner client statements should be responded to with simple affirmations, and the intermediate and advanced statements should be responded to with complex affirmations.

SKILL CRITERIA FOR EXERCISE 9

1. For the beginner client statements, use *simple affirmations* that express appreciation, encouragement, or reinforcement of the client's effort.
2. For the intermediate and advanced client statements, use *complex affirmations* that reflect the deeper meaning of the client's strengths or abilities.
3. All affirmations should be genuine and intentional.

Examples of Clinicians Using Affirmations

Example 1

CLIENT: [*concerned*] I don't know if this is the right place for me. I have never talked with anyone about my problems. I think I should be able to take care of my own business.

CLINICIAN: You made a good decision to come here today. (Simple Affirmation)

or

CLINICIAN: You have a strong sense of responsibility to take care of your problems yourself. (Complex Affirmation)

Example 2

CLIENT: [*frustrated*] I have been trying so hard to manage my blood sugar levels. I watch my diet and try to walk when I can. I'm so discouraged that it isn't working!

CLINICIAN: I want to applaud the efforts you have made! Good work. (Simple Affirmation)

or

CLINICIAN: You are dedicated to taking care of your health. (Complex Affirmation)

Example 3

CLIENT: [*exasperated*] I can't believe that I drank this week! I have been sober for almost a year. Now that is gone. I guess I will always be a drunk.

CLINICIAN: You went almost a whole year without drinking. That is amazing. (Simple Affirmation)

or

CLINICIAN: You have put in so much time and effort into your sobriety and you want it to count for something. (Complex Affirmation)

Example 4

CLIENT: [*annoyed*] That social media is so addictive! I can't seem to stay away from it. I have noticed though that there is a lot of nonsense stuff on there. It clutters the mind.

CLINICIAN: I would say noticing is a great first step to making a change. (Simple Affirmation)

or

CLINICIAN: You are really paying attention to the effect that social media has on you. (Complex Affirmation)

Example 5

CLIENT: [*frustrated*] My kids are driving me crazy. I get so frustrated with them when they don't behave. I keep trying to take a more positive approach, but it's hard to catch them being good!

CLINICIAN: You are continuing to try new positive approaches. (Simple Affirmation)

or

CLINICIAN: You are determined to deal with your kids in a positive way, helping them be good! (Complex Affirmation)

Example 6

CLIENT: [*exasperated*] I am so sick and tired of Zoom! Between trying to help my kids with school and keeping up with my own work, it's too much!

CLINICIAN: You have done some heroic work keeping up with all of the Zoom calls! (Simple Affirmation)

or

CLINICIAN: It might not feel like you have a choice, but you are choosing daily to stick with it despite the frustration. (Complex Affirmation)

INSTRUCTIONS FOR EXERCISE 9

Step 1: Role-Play and Feedback

- The client says the first beginner client statement. The clinician improvises a response based on the skill criteria.
- The trainer (or, if not available, the client) provides brief feedback based on the skill criteria.
- The client then repeats the same statement, and the clinician again improvises a response. The trainer (or client) again provides brief feedback.

Step 2: Repeat

- Repeat Step 1 for all the statements in the current difficulty level (beginner, intermediate, or advanced).

Step 3: Assess and Adjust Difficulty

- The clinician completes the Deliberate Practice Reaction Form (see Appendix A) and decides whether to make the exercise easier or harder or to repeat the same difficulty level.

Step 4: Repeat for Approximately 15 Minutes

- Repeat Steps 1 to 3 for at least 15 minutes.
- The trainees then switch clinician and client roles and start over.

Now it's your turn! Follow Steps 1 and 2 from the instructions.

Remember: The goal of the role-play is for trainees to practice improvising responses to the client statements in a manner that (a) uses the skill criteria and (b) feels authentic for the trainee. **Example clinician responses for each client statement are provided at the end of this exercise. Trainees should attempt to improvise their own responses before reading the example responses.**

Also remember: The clinician should respond to each of the beginner client statements with a simple affirmation and to each of the intermediate and advance client statements with a complex affirmation.

BEGINNER-LEVEL CLIENT STATEMENTS FOR EXERCISE 9
Beginner Client Statement 1
[Matter of fact] I finally got my homework done! It was a little late but at least it is in.
Beginner Client Statement 2
[Sad] I'm really having a hard time right now. I lost my father just a month ago and my mom is falling apart, and I don't seem much better.
Beginner Client Statement 3
[Motivated] I finished treatment! It feels pretty good. Maybe I'll be able to stay sober this time.
Beginner Client Statement 4
[Accomplished] I only used drugs a few times this week. That is a big change for me.
Beginner Client Statement 5
[Motivated] I really want to get my kids back. I know it will be a lot of work and I am all in.

Assess and adjust the difficulty before moving to the next difficulty level (see Step 3 in the exercise instructions).

INTERMEDIATE-LEVEL CLIENT STATEMENTS FOR EXERCISE 9

Intermediate Client Statement 1

[Frustrated] I just got diagnosed with diabetes. I can't believe it! I have been trying hard to avoid that diagnosis. I mean I don't eat sweets, and I try to exercise. It just isn't fair.

Intermediate Client Statement 2

[Exasperated] I just don't think I can quit smoking. The only time I was able to do that was when I was pregnant and had too much morning sickness to smoke! Too late to try that again!

Intermediate Client Statement 3

[Uncertain] I am so stressed out. I decided to go back to school. I love it, but I think I am in over my head. I just can't seem to keep up.

Intermediate Client Statement 4

[Concerned] This isolation is killing me! I miss seeing my friends and just getting out to meetings. I have done a few Zoom AA meetings and that has kept me sober. But I am eating myself to death now!

Intermediate Client Statement 5

[Motivated] Okay, so my new year's resolution is to turn off my phone or at least silence it an hour before I go to bed. I just couldn't pull myself away from it! I would be scrolling around way too late. I haven't been able to stop. I need to figure this out. All that scrolling keeps me awake.

Assess and adjust the difficulty before moving to the next difficulty level (see Step 3 in the exercise instructions).

ADVANCED-LEVEL CLIENT STATEMENTS FOR EXERCISE 9
Advanced Client Statement 1
[Uncertain] My anxiety levels are out of control these days! There is so much going on in the world that I have no control over and I am so afraid of. What is going to happen to us? I know I need to do something different, but I'm not sure what or even if I can do anything.
Advanced Client Statement 2
[Sad] I have to make a decision about my marriage. I am so unhappy but I know that I haven't done everything I could. My partner seems oblivious to what is happening. I just can't keep it up.
Advanced Client Statement 3
[Concerned] Last night my son came home drunk and really angry. I was there by myself, and it scared me. He's never gotten violent before, but I could see it in his eyes. I wish I knew how to help him!
Advanced Client Statement 4
[Motivated] Can you please help me get off this stuff? The doctors who got me hooked are now trying to take these pills away! I am so scared.
Advanced Client Statement 5
[Frustrated] Wouldn't you know it! They are blaming me for the fact that my knee replacement didn't work. They just yell at me about not doing the physical therapy enough. Well, that's because it hurts! I have been trying to do it, but it's hard when the pain is there.

🛑 **Assess and adjust the difficulty here (see Step 3 in the exercise instructions). If appropriate, follow the instructions to make the exercise even more challenging (see Appendix A).**

Example Therapist Responses: Affirmations

Remember: Trainees should attempt to improvise their own responses before reading the example responses. **Do not read the following responses verbatim unless you are having trouble coming up with your own responses!**

EXAMPLE RESPONSES TO BEGINNER-LEVEL CLIENT STATEMENTS FOR EXERCISE 9
Example Response to Beginner Client Statement 1
That's great that you got it done.
Example Response to Beginner Client Statement 2
You are working hard to keep it together.
Example Response to Beginner Client Statement 3
Finishing treatment is a great accomplishment.
Example Response to Beginner Client Statement 4
You were able to abstain for several days! That is great.
Example Response to Beginner Client Statement 5
You are willing to do the hard work.

EXAMPLE RESPONSES TO INTERMEDIATE-LEVEL CLIENT STATEMENTS FOR EXERCISE 9
Example Response to Intermediate Client Statement 1
You have already put in so much effort and time into taking care of yourself. You really care about your health.
Example Response to Intermediate Client Statement 2
When it was really important for you to quit, you were able to find the strength to do it.
Example Response to Intermediate Client Statement 3
You are committed to making school work for you.
Example Response to Intermediate Client Statement 4
You are doing what it takes to stay sober and dealing with the isolation.
Example Response to Intermediate Client Statement 5
You are determined to find a way to manage your phone time. You keep at it even when it is challenging.

EXAMPLE RESPONSES TO ADVANCED-LEVEL CLIENT STATEMENTS FOR EXERCISE 9
Example Response to Advanced Client Statement 1
You are hopeful that there is something that you can do differently that will help.
Example Response to Advanced Client Statement 2
You aren't willing to give up without giving it your best effort.
Example Response to Advanced Client Statement 3
You are determined to both stay safe and to do what you can to help.
Example Response to Advanced Client Statement 4
You really want to be free of the pills. It takes courage to ask for help.
Example Response to Advanced Client Statement 5
You keep trying even though it hurts! That takes determination.

Autonomy Support

Preparations for Exercise 10

1. Read the instructions in Chapter 2.

2. Download the Deliberate Practice Reaction Form and the Deliberate Practice Diary Form at https://www.apa.org/pubs/books/deliberate-practice-motivational-interviewing (see the "Clinician and Practitioner Resources" tab; also available in Appendixes A and B, respectively).

Skill Description

Skill Difficulty Level: Advanced

One of the underlying beliefs of motivational interviewing (MI) is that individuals have a right and responsibility for self-determination and self-governance. They have the capacity for being autonomous human beings. Supporting and encouraging the awareness and perception of autonomy in clients is one of the key skills used by clinicians. As with other skills, autonomy support has an internal, attitudinal component (belief in self-determination) and an external component that involves actively conveying that attitude to clients. The client's perception of autonomy can be influenced through several types of responses that explicitly acknowledge a client's personal choice or control in the situation. These responses fall into three categories:

1. Explicit statements regarding autonomy, personal choice, or control. For example:
   a. "The choice is yours and yours only."
   b. "It is really up to you to determine what, if anything, you would like to change."
   c. "No one can make you change your drinking. Only you can make that choice."

---

https://doi.org/10.1037/0000297-012

Deliberate Practice in Motivational Interviewing, by J. K. Manuel, D. Ernst, A. Vaz, and T. Rousmaniere

2. Questions that ask for the client to consider choices or determine the course. For example:

   a. "Of all of these possible options, what seems the best way for you?"

   b. "What are the things you can do to move in your chosen direction?"

   c. "What shall we do today to help you move forward?"

3. Reflections that emphasize the client's sense of choice. For example:

   a. "You are at a crossroads and trying to determine the right path for you."

   b. "You have a strong sense of responsibility to take care of your problems yourself."

   c. "You made a deliberate choice to become a more positive-oriented parent."

In MI, the clinician avoids responding in ways that decrease a sense of autonomy (e.g., "I can tell you the best way to take care of your problems is . . .") and instead offers responses that emphasize the client's choice and control in the situation.

Each type of response is increasingly difficult to formulate and deliver—that is, explicit statements are relatively easier to use than questions, which in turn are simpler than reflections. Therefore, each difficulty level in this exercise focuses on using just one of the three responses to promote client autonomy, as described in the skill criteria.

SKILL CRITERIA FOR EXERCISE 10

1. For the beginner client statements, respond with an *explicit statement* regarding autonomy, personal choice, or control.
2. For the intermediate client statements, respond with a *question* that asks for the client to consider choices or determine the course.
3. For the advanced client statements, respond with a *reflection* that emphasizes the client's sense of choice.
4. For all client statements, avoid offering advice, opinions, or other directive responses that could reduce the client's sense of autonomy.

Examples of Clinicians Using the Skill of Autonomy Support

Example 1: Using an Explicit Statement Regarding Autonomy, Personal Choice, or Control

CLIENT: [*exasperated*] I have given up so much for my family. They are pressuring me to quit smoking and I'm sick of it. I wish they would leave me alone!

CLINICIAN: Your family can pressure you, but in the end, it is really up to you what, if anything, you do about your smoking.

Example 2: Using a Question That Asks Clients to Consider Choices or Determine the Course

CLIENT: [*adamant*] I don't think vaccines are safe, and I'm not going to risk my health.

CLINICIAN: What would help you make a decision about the vaccine?

Example 3: Using a Reflection That Emphasizes the Client's Sense of Choice

CLIENT: [*frustrated*] I think this is ridiculous. My wife made me come here and threatened to leave me if I didn't. I don't need help.

Clinician: You feel a sense of responsibility to take care of your problems yourself.

INSTRUCTIONS FOR EXERCISE 10

Step 1: Role-Play and Feedback

- The client says the first beginner client statement. The clinician improvises a response based on the skill criteria.
- The trainer (or, if not available, the client) provides brief feedback based on the skill criteria.
- The client then repeats the same statement, and the clinician again improvises a response. The trainer (or client) again provides brief feedback.

Step 2: Repeat

- Repeat Step 1 for all the statements in the current difficulty level (beginner, intermediate, or advanced).

Step 3: Assess and Adjust Difficulty

- The clinician completes the Deliberate Practice Reaction Form (see Appendix A) and decides whether to make the exercise easier or harder or to repeat the same difficulty level.

Step 4: Repeat for Approximately 15 Minutes

- Repeat Steps 1 to 3 for at least 15 minutes.
- The trainees then switch clinician and client roles and start over.

> **Now it's your turn! Follow Steps 1 and 2 from the instructions.**

Remember: The goal of the role-play is for trainees to practice improvising responses to the client statements in a manner that (a) uses the skill criteria and (b) feels authentic for the trainee. **Example clinician responses for each client statement are provided at the end of this exercise. Trainees should attempt to improvise their own responses before reading the example responses.**

Also remember: The clinician should respond to each of the beginner client statements with an *explicit statement* regarding autonomy, personal choice, or control.

BEGINNER-LEVEL CLIENT STATEMENTS FOR EXERCISE 10
Beginner Client Statement 1
[Adamant] I don't like it when anyone tells me what to do.
Beginner Client Statement 2
[Exasperated] My husband is threatening to take the kids away if I don't get help. I don't think I need it.
Beginner Client Statement 3
[Matter of fact] My doctor says I don't have any choice but to quit. She says if I keep smoking, I will die.
Beginner Client Statement 4
[Adamant] The government has no right to tell me what I can and cannot do with my body! They are just trying to control me.
Beginner Client Statement 5
[Frustrated] I do want to get my diabetes under control. Just not sure how to get there. It can feel overwhelming.

✋ **Assess and adjust the difficulty before moving to the next difficulty level (see Step 3 in the exercise instructions).**

Remember: The clinician should respond to each of the intermediate client statements with a *question* that asks for the client to consider choices or determine the course.

INTERMEDIATE-LEVEL CLIENT STATEMENTS FOR EXERCISE 10
Intermediate Client Statement 1
[Matter of fact] I don't have any idea what you all do here. I expect you will just tell me what I have to do.
Intermediate Client Statement 2
[Exasperated] You are probably like all of the other treatments programs I have been to. Making me go to a 12-step program and having to do it your way.
Intermediate Client Statement 3
[Determined] I really need to decide about what to do with my marriage. I just keep going back and forth.
Intermediate Client Statement 4
[Frustrated] I just feel so trapped in my life. It's like everyone else is in charge.
Intermediate Client Statement 5
[Matter of fact] The only reason I am here is because the court forced me to come. It was here or jail.

Assess and adjust the difficulty before moving to the next difficulty level (see Step 3 in the exercise instructions).

Remember: The clinician should respond to each of the advanced client statements with a *reflection* that emphasizes the client's sense of choice.

ADVANCED-LEVEL CLIENT STATEMENTS FOR EXERCISE 10
Advanced Client Statement 1
[Motivated] This social media is taking over my life! It is just so addictive. I can't stand the feeling that I am not in control of it.
Advanced Client Statement 2
[Frustrated] My employer is trying to mandate that we get vaccinated. I think that is outrageous! Both my job and my health are important to me, but I really resent it.
Advanced Client Statement 3
[Frustrated] I need to learn how to choose my own way. It seems that I get sucked into everyone else's opinions and then just get carried away. I end up feeling bad!
Advanced Client Statement 4
[Matter of fact] My doctor wants me to take an antidepressant. I just feel like I should be able to deal with this on my own. It feels like a cop out to take pills.
Advanced Client Statement 5
[Exasperated] They are telling me that I have to take a driver's test before I can renew my license. Just because of my age. Doesn't seem fair. I would like to be in charge of when I quit driving rather than having it yanked away from me.

Assess and adjust the difficulty here (see Step 3 in the exercise instructions). If appropriate, follow the instructions to make the exercise even more challenging (see Appendix A).

Example Clinician Responses: Autonomy Support

Remember: Trainees should attempt to improvise their own responses before reading the example responses. **Do not read the following responses verbatim unless you are having trouble coming up with your own responses!**

EXAMPLE RESPONSES TO BEGINNER-LEVEL CLIENT STATEMENTS FOR EXERCISE 10
Example Response to Beginner Client Statement 1
Others may share their thoughts, although ultimately, this decision really is up to you.
Example Response to Beginner Client Statement 2
You are the only one who can decide what you do next.
Example Response to Beginner Client Statement 3
The choice about whether to change your smoking is yours. The doctor may express her concern, but you are the one to decide what, if anything, to do about your smoking.
Example Response to Beginner Client Statement 4
There are laws and rules, and it's up to you to decide if you want to adhere to them. You can weigh the costs of breaking the rules and decide what you want to do.
Example Response to Beginner Client Statement 5
I can share my thoughts, and it will be up to you to decide what, if any, changes you make.

EXAMPLE RESPONSES TO INTERMEDIATE-LEVEL CLIENT STATEMENTS FOR EXERCISE 10

Example Response to Intermediate Client Statement 1

What if I explained a bit about what we do here and how we work with people who come here?

Example Response to Intermediate Client Statement 2

There are definitely many options here for treatment. Would you like me to tell you a bit about those options?

Example Response to Intermediate Client Statement 3

What could we do that would help you with that decision?

Example Response to Intermediate Client Statement 4

What would it look like if you were in charge?

Example Response to Intermediate Client Statement 5

It seems that you have chosen to come here instead of going to jail. How did you make that decision?

EXAMPLE RESPONSES TO ADVANCED-LEVEL CLIENT STATEMENTS FOR EXERCISE 10
Example Response to Advanced Client Statement 1
You'd really like to have a sense of control over how you spend your time.
Example Response to Advanced Client Statement 2
You want to be in charge of the really tough decisions in your life, like whether to get vaccinated.
Example Response to Advanced Client Statement 3
You can see that you have your own unique path and you feel good when you are able to follow that.
Example Response to Advanced Client Statement 4
You have a strong sense of responsibility for your own health.
Example Response to Advanced Client Statement 5
You'd like to be the one to determine when it is time to give up driving. You don't want others to force that decision on you.

Agenda Mapping

Preparations for Exercise 11

1. Read the instructions in Chapter 2.

2. Download the Deliberate Practice Reaction Form and the Deliberate Practice Diary Form at https://www.apa.org/pubs/books/deliberate-practice-motivational-interviewing (see the "Clinician and Practitioner Resources" tab; also available in Appendixes A and B, respectively).

Skill Description

Skill Difficulty Level: Advanced

In motivational interviewing (MI), the target of change or focus of the conversation (e.g., quitting smoking, dietary change, treatment adherence) must be mutually agreed upon by the clinician and client. The overall target of change may be predetermined by the setting or context of the conversation, such as a client call to a Tobacco Quit Line or a client requesting treatment in a posttraumatic stress disorder clinic. Even when the overall target is evident or when there are many possible target changes, it is critical that the clinician and client come to agreement about the focus of the conversation at hand. Although MI is a client-centered approach, the clinician also brings requirements and professional judgment to the conversation. Agenda mapping is a relatively simple process of eliciting all possible agenda items from both the clinician and client. The clinician then facilitates prioritization of the items and suggests a time frame for managing the agenda. This is a collaborative process that honors the

---

https://doi.org/10.1037/0000297-013

Deliberate Practice in Motivational Interviewing, by J. K. Manuel, D. Ernst, A. Vaz, and T. Rousmaniere

expertise of the clinician and the lived experience of the client. The process consists of the following steps:

1. Elicit the client's concerns, potential topics, and possible areas of focus for the conversation.

2. Bring forth the clinician's agenda, which may include requirements of the service, basis of the referral to the service, essential topics included in the program, and the clinician's concerns or suggestions for the agenda.

3. Ask the client to prioritize their potential agenda items and possible areas of focus.

4. Offer a suggested agenda for the conversation, which includes the client's priority and the priority of the service and/or clinician, as well as a time allotted to each topic.

In this exercise, the clinician will be provided prompts throughout to practice these steps to continue the dialogue with the client.

SKILL CRITERIA FOR EXERCISE 11
See the clinician prompts within each dialogue for skill criteria.

Example of Clinician Using Agenda Mapping

EXAMPLE: PRIMARY CARE BEHAVIORAL HEALTH
The client is referred by the physician to a behavioral health specialist for a discussion about cannabis use.
CLINICIAN: What brings you here today?
CLIENT: [*motivated*] I was having my regular checkup with my primary care provider and she suggested I talk with you about a "lifestyle checkup." I don't know what that is, but I'm here!
CLINICIAN: 1. Reflect: A lifestyle checkup! Sounds interesting. 2. Elicit the client's concerns and potential topics for discussion: How about we start with you telling me about the concerns you have or what you would like to spend our time talking about.
CLIENT: [*motivated*] Well, I am having trouble with sleep, and she said you might be able to help with that.
CLINICIAN: 1. Reflect: So sleep is one we could discuss. 2. Ask for additional topics: What other topics might be useful to discuss?
CLIENT: [*determined*] I know I need to get out and move more. That would probably help my mood and my weight.
CLINICIAN: 1. Reflect: It sounds like moving more would have lots of benefits, including improved mood. 2. Ask for anything else the client might want to discuss: Anything else?
CLIENT: [*frustrated*] Well, she thinks I might be using too much pot. It really helps with sleep.
CLINICIAN: 1. Reflect: You find the pot helpful with your sleep issues. 2. Offer the agenda for referral—discuss cannabis use: The doctor did ask that we have a conversation about your cannabis use. I'd like to add that to the agenda. 3. Ask about the client's priorities: You have mentioned sleep issues, moving more, mood improvement, and weight as potential topics. When you think about those, is there one that stands out as a priority for our discussion today?
CLIENT: [*motivated*] I think the sleep. Especially if I have to start thinking about not using pot to help with that.
CLINICIAN: 1. Offer a tentative agenda: How about we spend half our time today on sleep and then the other half on pot? How does that sound?
CLIENT: [*agreeingly*] Makes sense to me.

INSTRUCTIONS FOR EXERCISE 11

Step 1: Role-Play With Clinician Improvisation

- The clinician initiates the dialogue by asking the client, "What brings you here today?" then the client reads the first beginning client statement.
- The client reads the next statement in the table. This continues until the dialogue has been completed.

Step 2: Feedback and Assess and Adjust Difficulty

- The trainer (or if not available, the client) provides brief feedback on the clinician's responses based on the skill criteria.
- The clinician completes the Deliberate Practice Reaction Form (see Appendix A) and decides whether to make the exercise easier or harder or to repeat the same dialogue.

Step 3: Repeat for Approximately 15 Minutes

- Repeat Steps 1 and 2 for at least 15 minutes.
- The trainees then switch clinician and client roles and start over.

Now it's your turn! Follow Steps 1 and 2 from the instructions.

Remember: The goal of the role-play is for trainees to practice improvising responses to the client statements in a manner that (a) uses the skill criteria and (b) feels authentic for the trainee. **Example clinician responses for each client statement are provided at the end of this exercise. Trainees should attempt to improvise their own responses before reading the example responses.**

BEGINNER-LEVEL DIALOGUE: GENERAL OUTPATIENT COUNSELING CENTER
CLINICIAN: What brings you here today?
CLIENT: [*exasperated*] My life is a mess! I don't even know where to start! I can't seem to catch a break and everyone is on my back.
CLINICIAN PROMPTS: 1. Reflect. 2. Elicit the client's concerns and potential topics for discussion.
CLIENT: [*concerned*] My husband is threatening to get a divorce and take the kids. I don't think he can, but it has me stressed out. I lost my job, and I am so depressed. I can't seem to snap out of it.
CLINICIAN PROMPTS: 1. Reflect. 2. Ask for additional potential topics.
CLIENT: [*motivated*] I really need to get a job. And one that pays enough to cover child care. I know that would help.
CLINICIAN PROMPTS: 1. Reflect. 2. Offer the clinician's agenda—screening for depression, substance use, suicide issues, and safety. 3. Ask about the client's priorities.
CLIENT: [*frustrated*] I think getting myself together to go out and find a job. It feels overwhelming.
CLINICIAN PROMPT: 1. Offer a tentative agenda that includes the client's priorities and the clinician's agenda.
CLIENT: [*motivated*] Okay, if you think it will help.

Assess and adjust the difficulty before moving to the next dialogue (see Step 2 in the exercise instructions).

INTERMEDIATE-LEVEL DIALOGUE:
CASE MANAGEMENT SERVICES FOR UNHOUSED INDIVIDUALS LIVING ON THE STREET OR IN TEMPORARY HOUSING

The client is mandated to see a behavioral health specialist to receive case management services.
CLINICIAN: What brings you here today?
CLIENT: [*exasperated*] Same old, same old. I need my bus pass. I can't get down to the day-hire place without it.
CLINICIAN PROMPTS: 1. Reflect. 2. Elicit the client's concerns and potential topics for discussion.
CLIENT: [*frustrated*] It is too darn hot! The shelter doesn't have any air-conditioning. Can I go to a different one? You know, it doesn't feel safe either. People take your stuff, and I can't get enough food.
CLINICIAN PROMPTS: 1. Reflect. 2. Ask for additional potential topics.
CLIENT: [*motivated*] I would like to find more work. It is so hard.
CLINICIAN PROMPTS: 1. Reflect. 2. Offer the clinician's agenda—required discussion about substance use. 3. Ask about the client's priorities.
CLIENT: [*determined*] I think I need to figure out how to stay safe in that place. That seems most important.
CLINICIAN PROMPT: 1. Offer a tentative agenda that includes the client's priorities and the clinician's agenda.
CLIENT: [*uncertain*] Okay, but I don't know if you can help.

✋ **Assess and adjust the difficulty before moving to the next dialogue (see Step 2 in the exercise instructions).**

ADVANCED-LEVEL DIALOGUE:
SUBSTANCE ABUSE TREATMENT AGENCY WITH A DIVERSION PROGRAM FOR PEOPLE WITH FIRST-TIME DRIVING UNDER THE INFLUENCE (DUI) CITATIONS

CLINICIAN: What brings you here today?
CLIENT: [*matter of fact*] I have to come. The court sent me.
CLINICIAN PROMPTS: 1. Reflect. 2. Elicit the client's concerns and potential topics for discussion.
CLIENT: [*exasperated*] Well, how to get the court off my back. I don't have a drinking problem, but they are making me not drink for the whole time I am here. So I guess we have to talk about that. What a bunch of BS.
CLINICIAN PROMPTS: 1. Reflect. 2. Ask for additional potential topics.
CLIENT: [*motivated*] I do have to figure out how to get this taken care of and still get to work every day. I can't afford to lose my job. I am scared about that. And I really didn't think I was drunk when I got stopped. I didn't even feel drunk!
CLINICIAN PROMPTS: 1. Reflect. 2. Offer the clinician's agenda—education about drinking and driving and support with working through court's requirements for the duration of program. 3. Ask about the client's priorities.
CLIENT: [*matter of fact*] Getting done with this.
CLINICIAN PROMPT: 1. Offer a tentative agenda that includes the client's priorities and the clinician's agenda.
CLIENT: [*matter of fact*] Okay.

Assess and adjust the difficulty here (see Step 2 in the exercise instructions). If appropriate, follow the instructions to make the exercise even more challenging (see Appendix A).

Example Clinician Responses: Agenda Mapping

Remember: Trainees should attempt to improvise their own responses before reading the example responses. **Do not read the following responses verbatim unless you are having trouble coming up with your own responses!**

EXAMPLE RESPONSES TO THE BEGINNER-LEVEL DIALOGUE: GENERAL OUTPATIENT COUNSELING CENTER
CLINICIAN: What brings you here today?
CLIENT: [*exasperated*] My life is a mess! I don't even know where to start! I can't seem to catch a break and everyone is on my back.
CLINICIAN: 1. Reflect: You're feeling pretty overwhelmed with everything going on. 2. Elicit the client's concerns and potential topics for discussion: What would be helpful for us to talk about today?
CLIENT: [*concerned*] My husband is threatening to get a divorce and take the kids. I don't think he can, but it has me stressed out. I lost my job, and I am so depressed. I can't seem to snap out of it.
CLINICIAN: 1. Reflect: So we could potentially talk about relationship issues, stress management, or depression. 2. Ask for additional potential topics: Anything else that concerns you that we might discuss?
CLIENT: [*motivated*] I really need to get a job. And one that pays enough to cover child care. I know that would help.
CLINICIAN: 1. Reflect: You would really like to get back to work. We'll add that to the list. 2. Offer the clinician's agenda: We routinely do some exploring of a variety of issues such as depression, substance use, and safety as part of our first visit. I would like to add it to the agenda. It also might help us figure out where to start. 3. Ask about the client's priorities: When you look at the list of your concerns, what stands out as most important to talk about today?
CLIENT: [*frustrated*] I think getting myself together to go out and find a job. It feels overwhelming.
CLINICIAN: 1. Offer a tentative agenda that includes the client's priorities and the clinician's agenda: How about we deal with the screening issues first and then spend the rest of our time together talking about finding work?
CLIENT: [*motivated*] Okay, if you think it will help.

EXAMPLE RESPONSES TO THE INTERMEDIATE-LEVEL DIALOGUE: CASE MANAGEMENT SERVICES FOR UNHOUSED INDIVIDUALS LIVING ON THE STREET OR IN TEMPORARY HOUSING

CLINICIAN: What brings you here today?

CLIENT: [*exasperated*] Same old, same old. I need my bus pass. I can't get down to the day-hire place without it.

CLINICIAN:
1. Reflect: You are interested in getting more work.
2. Elicit the client's concerns and potential topics for discussion: Tell me what other concerns that you have that we might discuss today?

CLIENT: [*frustrated*] It is too darn hot! The shelter doesn't have any air-conditioning. Can I go to a different one? You know, it doesn't feel safe either. People take your stuff, and I can't get enough food.

CLINICIAN:
1. Reflect: So things are kind of rough at the shelter, and you'd like to change that.
2. Ask for additional potential topics: What else would be helpful to discuss?

CLIENT: [*motivated*] I would like to find more work. It is so hard.

CLINICIAN:
1. Reflect: You'd like some help exploring how to get more work.
2. Offer the agenda of the service: As you know, we are required at every visit to check in about how it's going with the drinking. I need to add that to the agenda.
3. Ask about the client's priorities: As you look at the issues you raised, what is the top priority today?

CLIENT: [*determined*] I think I need to figure out how to stay safe in that place. That seems most important.

CLINICIAN:
1. Offer a tentative agenda that includes the client's priorities and the clinician's agenda: Makes sense. How about we spend most of our time on the safety issue and then check in about the drinking?

CLIENT: [*uncertain*] Okay, but I don't know if you can help.

EXAMPLE RESPONSES TO THE ADVANCED-LEVEL DIALOGUE: SUBSTANCE ABUSE TREATMENT AGENCY WITH A DIVERSION PROGRAM FOR PEOPLE WITH FIRST TIME DRIVING UNDER THE INFLUENCE (DUI) CITATIONS

CLINICIAN: What brings you here today?

CLIENT: [*matter of fact*] I have to come. The court sent me.

CLINICIAN:
1. Reflect: It wasn't your idea to come here.
2. Elicit the client's concerns and potential topics for discussion: What concerns do you have about the process? What would be helpful for you?

CLIENT: [*exasperated*] Well, how to get the court off my back. I don't have a drinking problem, but they are making me not drink for the whole time I am here. So I guess we have to talk about that. What a bunch of BS.

CLINICIAN:
1. Reflect: You are interested in clearing this up and getting back to your life.
2. Ask for additional potential topics: What else would be helpful to discuss?

CLIENT: [*motivated*] I do have to figure out how to get this taken care of and still get to work every day. I can't afford to lose my job. I am scared about that. And I really didn't think I was drunk when I got stopped. I didn't even feel drunk!

CLINICIAN:
1. Reflect: Sounds like it confused you when you got a DUI.

2. Offer the agenda of the service: This program includes education about alcohol and support with working through the court's requirements for the duration of this program.

3. Ask about the client's priorities: When you think about it, what seems to be the highest priority to discuss today?

CLIENT: [*matter of fact*] Getting done with this.

CLINICIAN:
1. Offer a tentative agenda that includes the client's priorities and the clinician's agenda: Got it! How about we spend most of our time looking at what it will take to complete the program successfully. Then we can talk a bit about your relationship with alcohol. What do you think?

CLIENT: [*matter of fact*] Okay.

Elicit–Provide–Elicit

Preparations for Exercise 12

1. Read the instructions in Chapter 2.

2. Download the Deliberate Practice Reaction Form and the Deliberate Practice Diary Form at https://www.apa.org/pubs/books/deliberate-practice-motivational-interviewing (see the "Clinician and Practitioner Resources" tab; also available in Appendixes A and B, respectively).

Skill Description

Skill Difficulty Level: Advanced

The exchange of information (e.g., providing information about why or how a client may engage in behavior change) between a clinician and clinician is **not** the primary mode of communication in a motivational interviewing (MI) conversation. There are, however, circumstances in which the clinician's expertise and knowledge might be helpful for the client in their decision making about how to make a particular behavior change. In MI, being able to provide information or share expertise in a collaborative and autonomy-supportive manner that doesn't overwhelm the client with information is considered a key skill. It is crucial that the clinician continue to use reflective listening and other MI-consistent skills throughout the discussion, acknowledging the client's knowledge, understanding, choice, and interest. It is important to remember that a lack of knowledge or information is **not** typically the reason for a client's ambivalence about making a behavior change. Therefore, clinicians should be thoughtful about why, how much, and in what way they are providing information to clients.

https://doi.org/10.1037/0000297–014
Deliberate Practice in Motivational Interviewing, by J. K. Manuel, D. Ernst, A. Vaz, and T. Rousmaniere

An MI-consistent way of providing information is Elicit–Provide–Elicit, which consists of the following steps:

1. **Elicit** can occur by (a) asking the client's permission to share information or (b) asking what the client already knows about the problem. At times, it may be appropriate to use both elicitation strategies, but often one or the other is sufficient.

   a. **Elicit the client's permission to share information.** This can occur if the client directly asks the provider for information ("Will the patch help with my cravings for cigarettes?"). Alternatively, a clinician can ask the client directly ("Would it be OK if I shared some ideas that have worked for other clients?") or to surround the information with statements that allow the client to choose how they receive the information ("I don't know if this will make sense to you, but you are the only one who decides if this fits for you").

   b. **Elicit the client's knowledge, understanding, or thoughts about the problem.** For example:

      • "What do you already know about the impact of drinking during pregnancy?"

      • "What are you already doing to make sure you get enough sleep?"

2. **Provide information** using neutral language and avoid any indicators that the client "should" take your suggestion or act on the information. "Less is more" applies to providing information. Limit the amount of information, be brief and concise, and tailor the information to what the client has said. For example:

   a. **Neutral language:** "The national recommendations regarding drinking and pregnancy indicate that there is no known safe amount of alcohol."

   b. **"Should" language (inconsistent with MI):** "There really is no amount of alcohol that is safe for you to drink during pregnancy. You need to stay away from drinking."

3. **Elicit the client's thoughts about the information**, encouraging them to process it. For example:

   a. "What do you make of this information?"

   b. "How, if at all, does this fit with your understanding?"

SKILL CRITERIA FOR EXERCISE 12

See the clinician prompts within each dialogue for skill criteria.

Example of Clinician Using Skill of Elicit–Provide–Elicit

EXAMPLE DIALOGUE: A CLIENT CONCERNED ABOUT SLEEP DIFFICULTIES
CLIENT: [*matter of fact*] I have had problems with getting enough sleep for most of my adult life. It is so hard to turn off my mind! I do find that a good stiff drink before bed does the trick, at least for getting to sleep.
CLINICIAN: 1. Reflect: You're interested in getting enough sleep and letting that mind rest. 2. Elicit the client's permission to share information: Would it be OK if I shared a bit of information on what we know about getting high-quality sleep?
CLIENT: [*agreeingly*] Sure.
CLINICIAN: 1. Reflect: You mentioned that drinking seems to help. 2. Elicit the client's knowledge: What have you heard or experienced about how alcohol affects your sleep?
CLIENT: [*matter of fact*] Like I said, it is helping me get to sleep. That was always a problem. I have to be careful though because I also know that if I have too much, it will cause me to wake up during the night and not be able to get back to sleep.
CLINICIAN: 1. Reflect: Well, you have already learned a lot about managing it. 2. Provide information: Sleep research does indicate that alcohol in the system does interfere with the sleep cycle and reduces the overall quality of the sleep. The recommendation is to not consume alcohol within the last couple of hours before going to bed. 3. Elicit the client's thoughts about the information: What thoughts do you have about that?
CLIENT: [*motivated*] It would be hard to give up that nightcap for sure! But I really do want to get better sleep. I feel so much better when I do.

INSTRUCTIONS FOR EXERCISE 12
Step 1: Role-Play With Clinician Improvisation
• The client reads the first beginning client statement. • The clinician improvises a response following the prompts in the table. • The client reads the next statement in the table. This continues until the dialogue has been completed.
Step 2: Feedback and Assess and Adjust Difficulty
• The trainer (or if not available, the client) provides brief feedback on the clinician's responses based on the skill criteria. • The clinician completes the Deliberate Practice Reaction Form (see Appendix A) and decides whether to make the exercise easier or harder or to repeat the same dialogue.
Step 3: Repeat for Approximately 15 Minutes
• Repeat Steps 1 and 2 for at least 15 minutes. • The trainees then switch clinician and client roles and start over.

> **Now it's your turn! Follow Steps 1 and 2 from the instructions.**

Remember: The goal of the role-play is for trainees to practice improvising responses to the client statements in a manner that (a) uses the skill criteria and (b) feels authentic for the trainee. **Example clinician responses for each client statement are provided at the end of this exercise. Trainees should attempt to improvise their own responses before reading the example responses.**

BEGINNER-LEVEL DIALOGUE: A CLIENT REFERRED FOR SMOKING CESSATION COUNSELING
CLIENT: [*concerned*] I know I should quit smoking. I've been doing it for too long. But I've tried quitting, and it didn't go so well. Do you really think there is a way to be successful at quitting?
CLINICIAN PROMPTS: 1. Reflect. 2. Elicit the client's knowledge and experience.
CLIENT: [*frustrated*] Well, I have seen advertisements about drugs. And I tried the nicotine gum last time. I couldn't stand the taste, and it just made me want to smoke. That's about all I know.
CLINICIAN PROMPTS: 1. Reflect. 2. Provide information about options—for example, new medications that help with cravings, a variety of nicotine replacement products, and support groups. 3. Ask what the client thinks about the information.
CLIENT: [*frustrated*] I think help with the craving would be good. Last time I tried, I just found myself craving all the time. And I would get irritable with everyone around me. I'm a little afraid of taking another drug . . .
CLINICIAN PROMPTS: 1. Reflect. 2. Provide a response that expresses confidence in the treatment, emphasizes the client's choice, and offers collaboration in the process.
Client: [*thoughtfully*] Maybe it is worth a try. It would help to hear more about those drugs.

Assess and adjust the difficulty before moving to the next dialogue (see Step 2 in the exercise instructions).

INTERMEDIATE-LEVEL DIALOGUE: A CLIENT UNSURE ABOUT TREATMENT ENGAGEMENT
CLIENT: [*exasperated*] I don't really know anything about this treatment thing. I mean, I feel like I should be able to take care of my own problems, and I am not even sure that drinking really is a problem for me.
CLINICIAN PROMPTS: 1. Reflect. 2. Ask permission to share information about options.
CLIENT: [*thoughtfully*] Yeah, I guess. You mean is there more than just going to those darn self-help groups like my wife keeps pushing?
CLINICIAN PROMPTS: 1. Reflect. 2. Provide information about options—for example, individual or group counseling, family programs, and educational classes. 3. Ask what the client thinks about the information.
CLIENT: [*curious*] Wow, that's a lot of different things. How do you decide what to do?
CLINICIAN PROMPTS: 1. Reflect. 2. Provide a response that emphasizes the client's choice and offers collaboration in the process.
CLIENT: [*interested*] Okay, I guess it wouldn't hurt to take a look at those. It will make my wife happy.

Assess and adjust the difficulty before moving to the next dialogue (see Step 2 in the exercise instructions).

ADVANCED-LEVEL DIALOGUE: A CLIENT REFERRED FOR AT-RISK DRINKING
CLIENT: [*cheerfully*] I've been hearing that red wine is really good for your heart. That makes me very happy. I make sure I get a few glasses every day!
CLINICIAN PROMPTS: 1. Reflect. 2. Ask permission to share information about guidelines for drinking, such as the National Institute on Alcohol Abuse and Alcoholism's (NIAAA's) guidelines.[1]
CLIENT: [*uncertain*] I guess so.
CLINICIAN PROMPTS: 1. Reflect. 2. Provide information about the NIAAA or other guidelines about drinking—no more than one drink a day for women or two drinks a day for men. 3. Ask what the client thinks about the information.
CLIENT: [*confused*] That doesn't really fit with what I have heard about the value of red wine. Besides, that doesn't seem like much at all!
CLINICIAN PROMPTS: 1. Reflect. 2. Provide a response that emphasizes the client's choice and offers collaboration in the process.
CLIENT: [*thoughtfully*] I guess I'll think about it. I don't want to harm myself, but I sure like that wine.

Assess and adjust the difficulty here (see Step 2 in the exercise instructions). If appropriate, follow the instructions to make the exercise even more challenging (see Appendix A).

---

1. The NIAAA's guidelines on drinking can be found here: https://www.niaaa.nih.gov/alcohol-health/ overview-alcohol-consumption/moderate-binge-drinking.

Example Clinician Responses: Elicit–Provide–Elicit

Remember: Trainees should attempt to improvise their own responses before reading the example responses. **Do not read the following responses verbatim unless you are having trouble coming up with your own responses!**

EXAMPLE RESPONSES TO THE BEGINNER-LEVEL DIALOGUE: A CLIENT REFERRED FOR SMOKING CESSATION COUNSELING
CLIENT: [*concerned*] I know I should quit smoking. I've been doing it for too long. But I've tried quitting, and it didn't go so well. Do you really think there is a way to be successful at quitting?
CLINICIAN: 1. Reflect: You've had some experience and you are looking for a way to be successful with quitting. 2. Elicit the client's knowledge and experience: What do you already know about the things out there to help people quit smoking?
CLIENT: [*frustrated*] Well, I have seen advertisements about drugs. And I tried the nicotine gum last time. I couldn't stand the taste, and it just made me want to smoke. That's about all I know.
CLINICIAN: 1. Reflect: The nicotine gum wasn't the one for you! 2. Provide information about options: There are many options. There are some new medications that help with cravings, some nicotine replacement products other than gum, and also support groups that can help people with quitting. 3. Ask what the client thinks about the information: What are your thoughts about those options?
CLIENT: [*frustrated*] I think help with the craving would be good. Last time I tried, I just found myself craving all the time. And I would get irritable with everyone around me. I'm a little afraid of taking another drug . . .
CLINICIAN: 1. Reflect: Getting help with the craving might make it a lot easier for you to consider quitting again. 2. Provide a response that expresses confidence in the treatment, emphasizes the client's choice, and offers collaboration in the process: I want you to know that these medications have been shown to be effective. Of course, the decision is always yours. I would be happy to explore them further if you would like.
CLIENT: [*thoughtfully*] Maybe it is worth a try. It would help to hear more about those drugs.

EXAMPLE RESPONSES FOR THE INTERMEDIATE-LEVEL DIALOGUE: A CLIENT UNSURE ABOUT TREATMENT ENGAGEMENT

CLIENT: [*exasperated*] I don't really know anything about this treatment thing. I mean, I feel like I should be able to take care of my own problems, and I am not even sure that drinking really is a problem for me.
CLINICIAN: 1. Reflect: You are committed to taking care of your problems. 2. Ask permission to share information about options: Would it be helpful if I shared some information about the options available here?
CLIENT: [*thoughtfully*] Yeah, I guess. You mean is there more than just going to those darn self-help groups like my wife keeps pushing?
CLINICIAN: 1. Reflect: You are concerned we might tell you the way to do this. 2. Provide information about options: We won't. There are several options here at the clinic. We offer individual and group counseling, family-oriented programs, and educational classes. 3. Ask what the client thinks about the information: I wonder what you think about those types of options?
CLIENT: [*curious*] Wow, that's a lot of different things. How do you decide what to do?
CLINICIAN: 1. Reflect: It seems like a lot of information to deal with. 2. Provide a response that emphasizes the client's choice and offers collaboration: You will be the one to choose which, if any, of the options you take. Would you like to take some time together to look more closely at the options?
CLIENT: [*interested*] Okay, I guess it wouldn't hurt to take a look at those. It will make my wife happy.

EXAMPLE RESPONSES TO ADVANCED-LEVEL DIALOGUE:
A CLIENT REFERRED FOR AT-RISK DRINKING

CLIENT: [*cheerfully*] I've been hearing that red wine is really good for your heart. That makes me very happy. I make sure I get a few glasses every day!

CLINICIAN:

1. Reflect: Sounds like you are committed to taking care of your health.
2. Ask permission to share information: Would it be okay if I shared the national guidelines for drinking safely?

CLIENT: [*uncertain*] I guess so.

CLINICIAN:

1. Reflect: You sound curious.
2. Provide information about guidelines: The guidelines are no more than one drink a day for women or two drinks a day for men.
3. Ask what the client thinks about the information: What do you make of that?

CLIENT: [*confused*] That doesn't really fit with what I have heard about the value of red wine. Besides, that doesn't seem like much at all!

CLINICIAN:

1. Reflect: You are surprised about the recommended amounts.

2. Provide a response that emphasizes the client's choice and offers collaboration in the process: Whether you choose to act on this information is completely up to you. I'd be happy to explore it further with you if you would like.

CLIENT: [*thoughtfully*] I guess I'll think about it. I don't want to harm myself, but I sure like that wine.

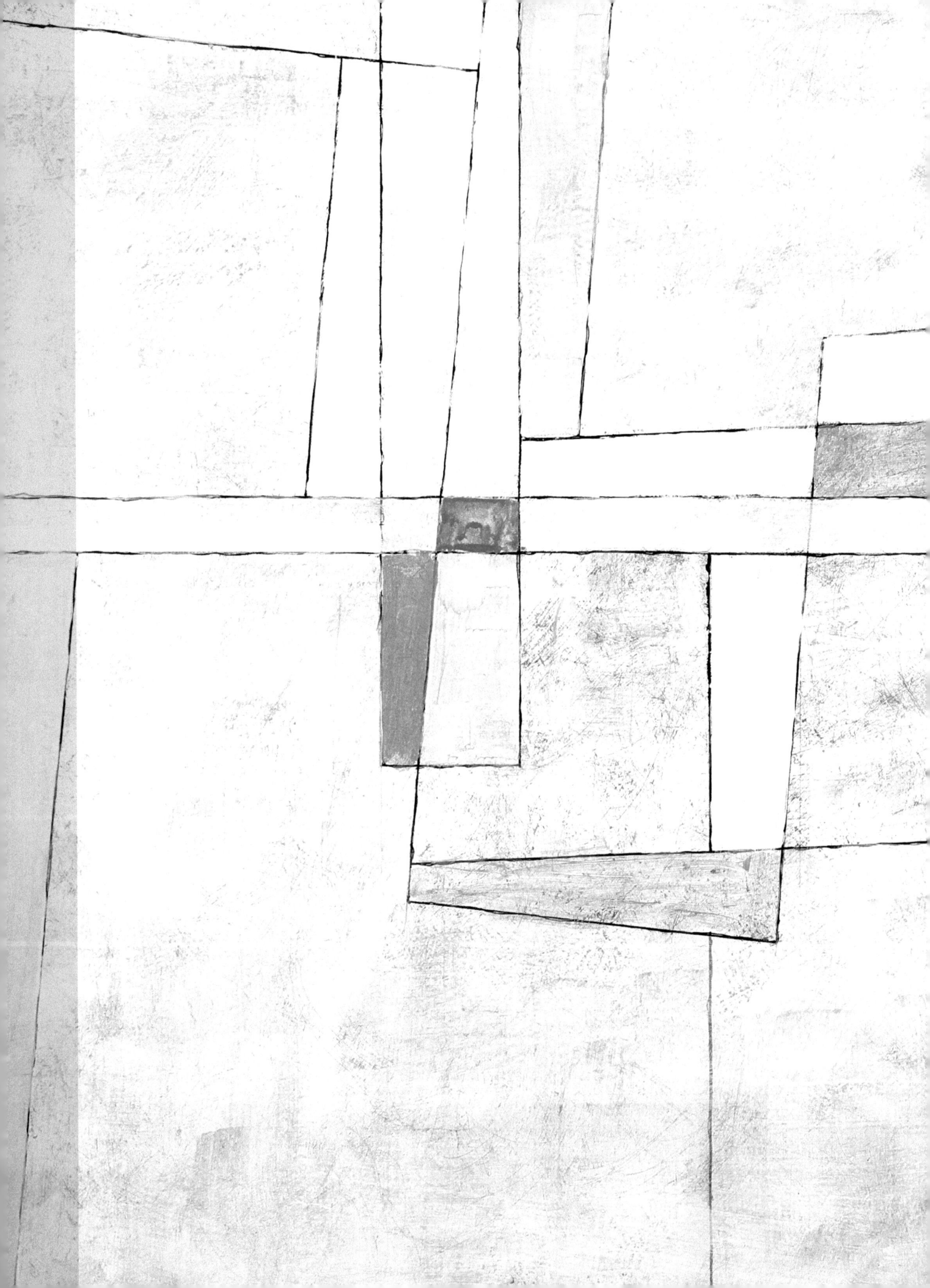

Annotated Motivational Interviewing Practice Session Transcript

It is now time to put together all the skills you have learned! This exercise presents a transcript from a typical brief motivational interviewing (MI) session in primary care. Each clinician statement is annotated to indicate which skill from Exercises 1 through 12 is used. This transcript provides an example of how clinicians can interweave many MI skills in response to clients.

Instructions

As in the previous exercises, one trainee can play the client while the other plays the clinician. As much as possible, the trainee who plays the client should try to adopt an authentic emotional tone as if they are a real client. The first time through, both partners can read verbatim from the transcript. After one complete run-through, try it again. This time, the client can read from the script while the clinician can improvise to the degree that they feel comfortable. At this point, you may also want to reflect upon it with a supervisor and go through it again. Before you start, it is recommended that both clinician and client read the entire transcript through on their own, until the end. The purpose of the sample transcript is to give trainees the opportunity to try out what it is like to offer the responses in a sequence that mimics a live MI session.

Note

In the following sample transcript, **client change talk** is highlighted in bold, whereas client sustain talk is underlined.

---

https://doi.org/10.1037/0000297-015

Deliberate Practice in Motivational Interviewing, by J. K. Manuel, D. Ernst, A. Vaz, and T. Rousmaniere

Annotated MI Transcript

The clinician in the transcript is a behavioral health specialist in a primary care clinic who takes referrals from providers for mental health, chronic disease management, substance use issues, and lifestyle issues. The client is a 48-year-old woman being treated for depression. She is presenting to the primary care clinic with sleep and mood problems.

CLINICIAN 1: Hello, I'm Sarah, the behavioral health specialist here at the clinic. Welcome. I see that Dr. Sloane suggested you stop by to see me. Tell me, what made you decide to take her up on that suggestion? (Skill 4: Reflections and Open-Ended Questions)

CLIENT 1: Dr. Sloane thought that you might be able to help me with my depression. I have been taking the medication she prescribed for about a year. I think that my mood really improved with the meds, and it was going pretty well. But now I feel like I am back at the beginning. Everything seems a mess.

CLINICIAN 2: You've been diligent in treating the depression and had some success to start with. (Skill 9: Complex Affirmation) What is happening now that you are concerned about? (Skill 4: Reflections and Open-Ended Questions)

CLIENT 2: It all started to fall apart when my mom died suddenly about 2 months ago. She was only 72, and she was my biggest support. I feel pretty lost without her. And my dad is no help.

CLINICIAN 3: It is a big loss that you are struggling to come to terms with. (Skill 2: Complex Reflection)

CLIENT 3: Yeah. I wasn't ready.

CLINICIAN 4: It was a big shock, and it's understandable and normal that you are struggling. (Skill 2: Complex Reflection) You mentioned that things have changed with your depression. Tell me what is concerning you about that. (Skill 11: Agenda Mapping—elicit the client's concerns and potential topics)

CLIENT 4: Well, I came in to see the doctor because I'm not sleeping well at all. And that means that I feel pretty exhausted most of the time. I don't seem to be able to get anything done.

CLINICIAN 5: Sounds like sleep management is something we could talk about together. (Skill 1: Simple Reflection). What else do you think it would be helpful to work on? (Skill 11: Agenda Mapping—ask for additional topics)

CLIENT 5: The doctor asked me about alcohol, which surprised me a bit. I'm not much of a drinker, but I have been drinking a bit more since mom died. And actually, my husband mentioned something to me about it as well.

CLINICIAN 6: So it might be helpful to discuss the role of alcohol in the depression and the grieving. (Skill 2: Complex Reflection) What else? (Skill 11: Agenda Mapping—ask for additional topics)

CLIENT 6: I have to figure out how to deal with dad. He is a basket case. You probably can't help with that.

CLINICIAN 7: You have several things, including sleep, alcohol, and some relationship issues with your dad. (Skill 1: Simple Reflection) Would it be alright if I shared some thoughts about additional items to discuss? (Skill 11: Agenda Mapping—offer the agenda of the clinician)

CLIENT 7: Sure.

CLINICIAN 8: I would like to suggest a discussion of resources that might be available to help you with your grieving. (Skill 11: Agenda Mapping—offer the agenda of the clinician) What do you think? (Skill 4: Reflections and Open-Ended Questions)

CLIENT 8: OK.

CLINICIAN 9: If you think about the potential items to discuss, does anything stand out as a priority or place you would like to start? (Skill 11: Agenda Mapping—ask about the client's priorities)

CLIENT 9: Well, the doctor gave me something today that is supposed to help with my sleep. And I think I just need to spend some time with my dad, as hard as that is. I guess the alcohol would be helpful because the doctor seemed to think that it might be contributing to my sleep problems.

CLINICIAN 10: How about we spend the first part of time together talking about the drinking and then spend some time talking about the resources for help with the grieving? (Skill 11: Agenda Mapping—offer a tentative agenda that includes the client's priorities and the clinician's agenda)

CLIENT 10: Sounds good.

CLINICIAN 11: Why don't you tell me about your perspective on the drinking? (Skill 4: Open-Ended Question)

CLIENT 11: Like I said, I have never been a big drinker. Well, except in my younger days in college. But I do like a good wine on special occasions. And I have to say that I appreciate a good whiskey also. I grew up in whiskey country and that was always a part of our family celebrations. What I have been doing lately is having a whiskey nightcap. I sit by myself and talk to my mom. Sounds crazy but <u>it feels good</u>. Sometimes I spend a couple of hours before bed, since I have such a hard time getting to sleep anyway, just talking with her.

CLINICIAN 12: In a way, the whiskey keeps you connected with your mom. It is a way of celebrating her. (Skill 2: Complex Reflection)

CLIENT 12: <u>I guess so</u>, but I usually have a good cry with it as well! If I have one too many, I end up in a puddle.

CLINICIAN 13: What do you think leads the doctor—or for that matter, your husband—to express concern about the drinking? (Skill 5: Elicit Change Talk—Open-Ended Question)

CLIENT 13: My husband just can't handle the tears. He thinks I should be over this by now. **The doctor said that it could be interfering with my sleep and my mood.**

CLINICIAN 14: So it could be having some unintended consequences for you. And you might have some concerns of your own. (Skill 6: Change Talk—Complex Reflection)

CLIENT 14: It does scare me a little. I can see how easy it would be to fall down the hole. I am watching my father try to drink himself to death, and it isn't pretty. There has been more than one family member who did that. I really don't want that!

CLINICIAN 15: You recognize the possible danger of allowing the drinking to go unchecked. (Skill 6: Change Talk—Complex Reflection)

CLIENT 15: I do see it and have always kept watch before now.

CLINICIAN 16: Sounds like a commitment to yourself to stay out of trouble with alcohol. (Skill 9: Complex Affirmation) I wonder what you already know about the connection between alcohol and sleep or mood? (Skill 12: Elicit–Provide–Elicit—elicit the client's knowledge)

CLIENT 16: I do know that alcohol is a depressant so it wouldn't help with my mood. Probably makes me feel worse if I drink too much. I've always thought that it helps with sleep. Makes it so much easier to fall asleep!

CLINICIAN 17: Alcohol has been helpful for falling asleep. (Skill 1: Simple Reflection) Would you like a bit more information about how it affects sleep? (Skill 12: Elicit–Provide–Elicit—elicit the client's permission to share information)

CLIENT 17: OK.

CLINICIAN 18: Alcohol, particularly drinking at night before going to bed, is known to interrupt one's sleep. While it may be helpful for falling asleep, it might wake a person up and make it more difficult to return to sleep. So the recommendation is to not have alcohol for at least 2 hours before going to bed. What do you think about that? (Skill 12: Elicit–Provide–Elicit—provide information; elicit the client's thoughts about the information)

CLIENT 18: I have experienced that at times when I have had too much to drink, like at a party or something. But I never thought that my nightcap might do that. My mom always swore by that nightcap! She would say it made for a peaceful night. **I guess she wasn't always right. Maybe I could have it earlier. Talk to her during happy hour.**

CLINICIAN 19: You are thinking that maybe the nightcap isn't the best way to get good sleep. The decision about if and when you have alcohol is yours to make. (Skill 10: Autonomy Support—explicit statement regarding autonomy, personal choice, or control) Is there anything else you would like to know to help you with that decision? (Skill 12: Elicit–Provide–Elicit—elicit the client's knowledge, understanding, or thoughts about the problem)

CLIENT 19: No, I don't think I am quite ready to give it up yet, **but I will plan on doing that soon.**

CLINICIAN 20: Sounds like you have already made the decision that it would be best in the long run to not have the nightcap. Probably not now and yet in the foreseeable future, you see that for yourself. (Skill 7: Double-Sided Reflection)

CLIENT 20: Yeah. I know it isn't good for me.

CLINICIAN 21: Let me see if I got this. You find yourself regularly having a nightcap that seems to connect you with your mom who you miss dearly. You're concerned that the extra alcohol might be interfering with your sleep and mood. You are watching your dad use alcohol to manage his grief, and it scares you a bit. You really care about your health and well-being and have always kept watch over your drinking. You see yourself letting go of that nightcap soon. Does that cover it? (Summary; series of reflections including Skills 1, 2, 3, 6, and 7)

CLIENT 21: Yes. Mom would want me to do that as well. She always worried about my dad's drinking.

CLINICIAN 22: Could we switch gears and talk about how you are doing with grieving?

CLIENT 22: Sure. I have to say that the grief just feels overwhelming at times. I miss her so much, and I'm kinda angry at her for leaving so suddenly. That sounds bad, doesn't it?

CLINICIAN 23: You feel bad about being a bit angry. (Skill 1: Simple Reflection) I have to say that anger is a very normal part of the grieving process. What are your thoughts about where you are in this? (Skill 4: Open-Ended Question)

CLIENT 23: It has really thrown me for a loop! And I would have thought that my dad and my husband would be supportive and also miss her. It is like they are on a different planet, both of them.

CLINICIAN 24: What would you think about getting some help with managing the grief? (Skill 4: Open-Ended Question)

CLIENT 24: I have been thinking about talking with my pastor about it. He has been helpful with other things. But I have been afraid of going back to church with the virus and everything.

CLINICIAN 25: Finding some meaningful support feels like it would be helpful. (Skill 6: Complex Reflection of Change Talk)

CLIENT 25: Yeah it does. I probably need to talk to someone else besides mom.

CLINICIAN 26: Would you be interested in hearing about some of the resources available for this? (Skill 12: Elicit–Provide–Elicit—elicit the client's permission to share information)

CLIENT 26: Sure.

CLINICIAN 27: The clinic hosts grief support groups for anyone in this situation. They have some that meet in person and some online. Sometimes it helps to talk with others who are experiencing grief. What are your thoughts about that? (Skill 12: Elicit–Provide–Elicit—provide information; elicit the client's thoughts about the information)

CLIENT 27: That sounds interesting. Particularly the online ones. I don't think I have it in me to go into the clinic regularly.

CLINICIAN 28: The support group is a possibility. There is also the option of doing some one-on-one therapy with one of our counselors. We have a couple who specialize in grief counseling. Finally, should you find that the grief continues to be overwhelming, there are more structured therapies that are shown to help people with what is called complicated grief. How do those sound? (Skill 12: Elicit–Provide–Elicit—provide information; elicit the client's thoughts about the information)

CLIENT 28: I don't think I should need anything that intense. It feels overwhelming just to think about it! But it is good to know it is there. **I think I will start by calling my pastor. The church might even have something that would help.** My mom was really active in the church.

CLINICIAN 29: You are going to start by making that call. (Skill 1: Simple Reflection) Is that something you think you could do in the next week or so? (Skill 5: Eliciting Change Talk)

CLIENT 29: I think so. I really feel the need to talk with someone.

CLINICIAN 30: Good. Would it be helpful if we set another time to check in about how that is going? We could explore other options if you felt like you need them.

CLIENT 30: I think that would be good.

CLINICIAN 31: Great. Let's set that up. Thank you so much for deciding to come in today. I know that it takes a lot in your situation to do this, and I appreciate it. (Skill 9: Complex Affirmation)

CLIENT 31: I'm glad I came.

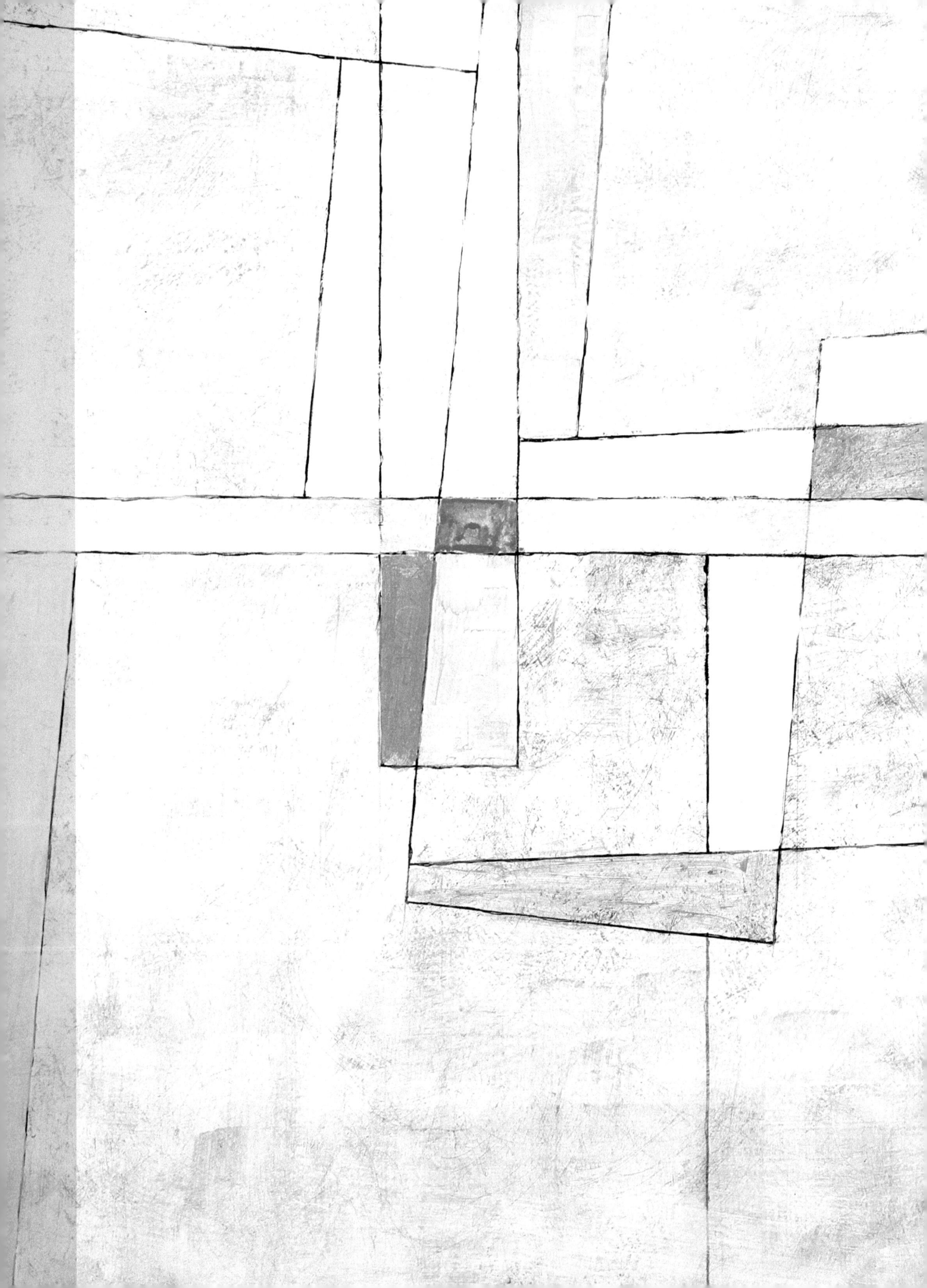

Mock Motivational Interviewing Sessions

In contrast to highly structured and repetitive deliberate practice exercises, a mock motivational interviewing (MI) session is an unstructured and improvised role-play MI session. Like a jazz rehearsal, mock sessions let you practice the art and science of *appropriate responsiveness* (Hatcher, 2015; Stiles & Horvath, 2017), putting your MI skills together in a way that is helpful to your mock client. This exercise outlines the procedure for conducting a mock MI session. It offers different client profiles you may choose to adopt when enacting clients. The last recommendation gives you the option to play yourself, a choice we have found to be highly rewarding.

Mock sessions are also an opportunity for trainees to practice the following:

- using MI skills responsively
- listening and forming deeper reflections
- differentiating change talk from other forms of client speech
- choosing when and how to respond to client language
- allowing the client's responses to influence the clinician's responses
- guiding the conversation toward change in a strategic way
- collaboratively focusing the conversation
- providing information in an autonomy supportive manner

Mock MI Session Overview

For the mock session, **you will perform a role-play of an MI conversation**. As is true with the exercises to build individual skills, the role-play involves three people: One trainee role-plays the clinician, another trainee role-plays the client, and a trainer (a professor or a supervisor) observes and provides feedback. This is an open-ended role-play, as is commonly done in training. However, this differs in three important ways from the role-plays used in more traditional training:

1. The clinician will use their hand to indicate how difficult the role-play feels.
2. The client will attempt to make the role-play easier or harder to ensure the clinician is practicing at the right difficulty level.

https://doi.org/10.1037/0000297-016
Deliberate Practice in Motivational Interviewing, by J. K. Manuel, D. Ernst, A. Vaz, and T. Rousmaniere

3. The trainer will provide specific feedback on MI skills, both what the clinician did well and one suggestion for improvement.

Preparation

1. Read the instructions in Chapter 2.

2. Download the Deliberate Practice Reaction Form and the Deliberate Practice Diary Form at https://www.apa.org/pubs/books/deliberate-practice-motivational-interviewing (see the "Clinician and Practitioner Resources" tab; also available in Appendixes A and B, respectively).

3. Designate one trainee to role-play the clinician and one trainee to role-play the client. The trainer will observe and provide feedback.

4. Every person will need their own copy of the Deliberate Practice Reaction Form on a separate piece of paper so they can access it quickly.

Mock MI Session Procedure

1. The trainees will role-play a MI conversation. The trainee designated as the clinician may choose one of the client profiles for specific skill practice (e.g., Agenda Mapping, Elicit–Provide–Elicit) or another profile may be chosen for general MI skill practice.

2. Before beginning the role-play, the clinician raises their hand to their side, at the level of their chair seat (see Figure E14.1). They will use this hand throughout the whole

FIGURE E14.1. Ongoing Difficulty Assessment Through Hand Level

Note. Left: Start of role-play. Right: Role-play is too difficult. From *Deliberate Practice in Emotion-Focused Therapy* (p. 156), by R. N. Goldman, A. Vaz, and T. Rousmaniere, 2021, American Psychological Association (https://doi.org/10.1037/0000227-000). Copyright 2021 by the American Psychological Association.

role-play to indicate how challenging it feels to them to help the client. Their starting hand level (chair seat) indicates that the role-play feels easy. By raising their hand, the clinician indicates that the difficulty is rising. If their hand rises above their neck level, it indicates that the role-play is too difficult.

3. The clinician begins the role-play. The clinician and client should engage in the role-play in an improvised manner, as they would engage in a real MI session. The clinician keeps their hand out at their side throughout this process. (This may feel strange at first!)

4. Whenever the clinician feels that the difficulty of the role-play has changed significantly, they should move their hand up if it feels more difficult; down if it feels easier. If the clinician's hand drops below the seat of their chair, the client should make the role-play more challenging; if the clinician's hand rises above their neck level, the client should make the role-play easier.

5. The role-play continues for at least 15 minutes. If the clinician gets significantly off-track, the trainer may request permission to provide corrective feedback during this process. However, trainers should exercise restraint and keep feedback as short and tight as possible because this will reduce the clinician's opportunity for experiential training.

6. After the role-play is finished, the clinician and client switch roles and begin a new mock session.

7. After both trainees have completed the mock session as a clinician, the trainees and the trainer discuss the experience.

Tips for Clinicians

- Each mock session is an opportunity to deepen your reflective listening skills. Reflections should be the most prevalent response and can include reflecting the client's emotional and voice tone.

- Practice listening closely to the client's language, deciding when and how to respond to change talk.

- Slow down, there is no need to rush through the conversation.

- Getting stuck is likely. Learn to recognize it. Usually, deeper reflections, including double-sided reflections ending in change talk, can get you unstuck. You may ask for help if you need it.

Tips for Clients

- Respond naturally to the clinician's efforts; if they ask for change talk, give it. Allow their response to influence your response.

- Don't get stuck in the details of the role you are playing. You can improvise.

- To vary the level of challenge,
  - increase difficulty by expressing more ambivalence with more emotional intensity and lots of sustain talk or
  - decrease difficulty by expressing less ambivalence, favoring change talk, and less intensity.

Tips for Trainers and Supervisors

- Intervene if
    - the clinician asks for help or
    - you get the permission of the clinician to step in if things are going off-track.
- The primary intervention used is to support deeper reflective listening and attention to change talk.
- Ask the clinician what they would like feedback on.
- Pay close attention to what the clinician does well in the conversation.
- Prioritize suggestions for improvement and pick **one**.
- Give very specific feedback focused on MI skills and delivered in a MI-consistent manner.

Mock Session Client Profiles

Following are six client profiles for trainees to use during mock sessions. The first four profiles are for beginning and intermediate practice of general MI skills. Profiles 5 and 6 are for practicing the advanced skills of Agenda Mapping and Elicit–Provide–Elicit. After these profiles is a third advanced profile in which clients have the option of playing themselves. The choice of client profile may be determined by the trainee playing the clinician, the trainee playing the client, or assigned by the trainer.

Beginner Profile: Working With a Client Who Wants to Quit Smoking

Paul is a 54-year-old delivery driver who smokes about 15 cigarettes per day. He smokes in the car as a way of breaking up the time spent driving. He's smoked for 35 years. He has quit smoking twice in the past, once when he was 40 years old and another time when he was 50 years old. In both instances, he quit smoking on his own, without the help of any medications or other support. He quit for about a month the first time and 6 months the second time. In both instances, he began smoking again while out with friends who smoke.

Goal of the Session

Explore the client's motivation and build confidence in his ability to quit smoking. He has called the tobacco quit line asking for help and was referred to the clinician's institution.

Reasons to Change

- The cost of cigarettes limits how much he can spend on other activities.
- He's worried about the health effects. His mother died of lung cancer at 62 years old.
- He had fewer headaches and slept better when he wasn't smoking.

Reasons Not to Change

- Paul is frustrated with prior relapses.
- He is not sure that anything can help him quit smoking.
- What would he do when out with a friend who smokes?

Emotional Responses

- Paul is worried about dying from lung cancer.
- He's angry that he's addicted to cigarettes.
- He's embarrassed by his smoking.

Beginner Profile: Reducing Alcohol Consumption in a Primary Care Setting

Marco is a 68-year-old married and recently retired man. He's been drinking more since retirement, usually several drinks a day. His wife asked him to talk with his physician about his drinking. She is concerned that drinking might cause him problems down the line. Marco's wife is important to him, so he did speak with his doctor. Marco has considered reducing how much he drinks, but he is adamant that he does not want to quit entirely.

Goal of the Session

As a behavioral health specialist in a primary care clinic, you have been asked to talk with Marco about drinking and what, if anything, he might like to change about it.

Reasons to Change

- His wife is unhappy with his drinking, he doesn't want her to be upset with him.
- He wants to be healthy and had planned to increase healthy activities when he retired.

Reasons Not to Change

- Marco enjoys drinking, and it helps him relax.
- Marco hasn't experienced the consequences, legal problems, or blackouts that he thinks would indicate his drinking was a problem.

Emotional Responses

- Marco is lonely. Retirement is not what he expected it to be.
- He's worried that his wife will become more and more frustrated with him.

Intermediate Profile: Improving Sleep Habits With a Reluctant Student

Jill is a 20-year-old college student who came to the Student Health Center reporting problems sleeping and waves of anxiety. At her first session, she talked about how she had difficulty falling asleep and getting up for her morning classes. She is a good student but has started falling behind a bit. In the discussion about her sleep habits, Jill indicated that she goes to bed with her phone and spends time on social media while she is trying to go to sleep.

Goal of the Session

Somewhat reluctantly, Jill agreed in the first session to have a conversation with you to explore and possibly resolve her ambivalence about disconnecting from social media at least an hour before bedtime.

Reasons to Change

- Jill wants to do well in her classes and needs to be alert and awake to do that.
- She has found that sometimes what comes across on social media makes her more anxious.

Reasons Not to Change

- Social media is the way Jill keeps in touch with her friends.
- She has been going to bed with her phone ever since she got her own phone and can't imagine not doing that final check each night.

Emotional Responses

- Jill is starting to get anxious that she won't do well in her classes, which are much harder this year.
- Jill is lonely and really misses her boyfriend who is gone for the term.

Intermediate Profile: A Client Who Is Hesitant About Changing Their Drinking Behaviors

Teresa is a 29-year-old single woman who works in advertising. She usually drinks weekend nights and will have several (six or more) cocktails. She often blackouts and has terrible hangovers. She once awoke in the back of her car in a strange part of town. She was very sick and ended up in urgent care. She has no memory of what happened or how she ended up in the back of her car.

Goal of the Session

Teresa has agreed to talk with someone about drinking, which was suggested by the provider. She is insistent that she is not an alcoholic. You are seeing her in the exam room to have the conversation.

Reasons to Change

- Her father was a heavy drinker, and she had to take care of him when he was sick. She is tired of being sick herself.
- She worries about getting into trouble with drinking.

Reasons Not to Change

- Teresa really enjoys drinking with her friends.
- Teresa views her drinking as normal.
- She does not drink alone, which she views as a sign of a drinking problem.

Emotional Responses

- Teresa is anxious in social situations and drinks to reduce her anxiety.
- This most recent blackout really scared her. She is not sure what she did.

Advanced Profile: Using the Elicit–Provide–Elicit Technique for Anger Management

Adrian is a 39-year-old man working in construction. He was sent to the Employee Assistance Program following an incident at work that involved a physical altercation with a coworker. He is required to go through the program and follow the recommendations. Adrian is married with two children, aged 11 and 14. He was hot-tempered as a teenager and had trouble with fighting. Adrian has engaged in no other physical violence as an adult besides this incident at work. He believes the other person was responsible for the altercation.

Goal of the Session

Using Elicit–Provide–Elicit, collaboratively explore the options available to the client (one-on-one sessions with a counselor, anger management classes, and mediation with the other party) and determine the course of action.

Reasons to Change

- Adrian enjoys and needs his job. He appreciates that he wasn't fired and is willing to do what it takes to keep it.

- Adrian grew up with a father who used physical violence to discipline him. He swore he would never be like that.

Reasons Not to Change

- He thinks that giving in to the other person involved would make him look weak.
- Adrian felt like his anger was out of his control and justified.

Emotional Responses

- Adrian is afraid about being out of control and reacting.
- He worries that it will happen again, and maybe with his kids.

Advanced Profile: Agenda Mapping for Diabetes Management

Liz is a 49-year-old woman diagnosed with type 2 diabetes. She has a family history of diabetes. When first diagnosed, she made major changes in her lifestyle, watching her diet closely and starting a regular walking program. She is married with three grown children and one new grandchild. Liz walked with her neighbor who recently moved to another town. Liz thinks the lack of walking is probably what is causing the problems with the diabetes. She has also pretty much quit monitoring her blood sugar because the results are depressing.

Goal of the Session

Check in about the behavioral components of diabetes management (physical activity, dietary changes, smoking, blood sugar monitoring, and stress management) and to collaboratively identify a focus for the conversation using agenda mapping (Skill 11). The physician has asked that you specifically discuss blood sugar monitoring.

Reasons to Change

- Liz doesn't want the complications of diabetes that her father had.
- Liz wants to be healthy to stay involved with her family.

Reasons Not to Change

- Liz is experiencing some depression and a sense of futility.
- Liz is certain that no one can replace her former walking partner.

Emotional Responses

- Liz experiences a sense of loss about her strength and ability to manage her diabetes.
- Liz is somewhat hopeful that she can get the diabetes back in control.

Advanced Profile: Play Yourself

The last example suggests that clinicians in training play themselves. In MI, this is called *real play*. This is considered the best way to develop a deeper understanding of MI. This allows one playing themselves as the client to experience how an MI conversation about change is different from other conversations and how collaboration and empathy feel from the client perspective. It also provides the practicing clinician to work with actual material and real issues, leading to a more authentic experience. In addition, getting feedback directly from a real client enhances the learning of the clinician. One important note here is that the person playing the client should choose a personal issue or topic that they feel comfortable exploring and deepening. Do not choose a topic that feels too evocative, traumatic, or dangerous to disclose and explore. The topic here is a change that you have been considering making but haven't decided to pursue. It will be something you are ambivalent about. It might be a change that would be "good for you," you "should" make for some reason, or perhaps have been putting off. The client needs to monitor their own experience and choose how deep they wish to go. Finally, in this particular exercise, it is not recommended for the therapist to use their hand as it could be distracting to the client and prevent exploration.

Instructions

Work in pairs. Using all of the MI skills, the clinician will conduct a 15-minute real play. This is done in the same manner as the other mock sessions except that there is not a supervisor or trainer participating. The client will be asked to provide feedback to the clinician about their experience after the interview. This feedback should include what was helpful and anything that was unhelpful. If both parties would like to, the interview may be done again to take into account the feedback. After completion of the first real play, change roles and conduct the second one. It is also suggested that the interviews are recorded (with permission of both parties) for further review and evaluation.

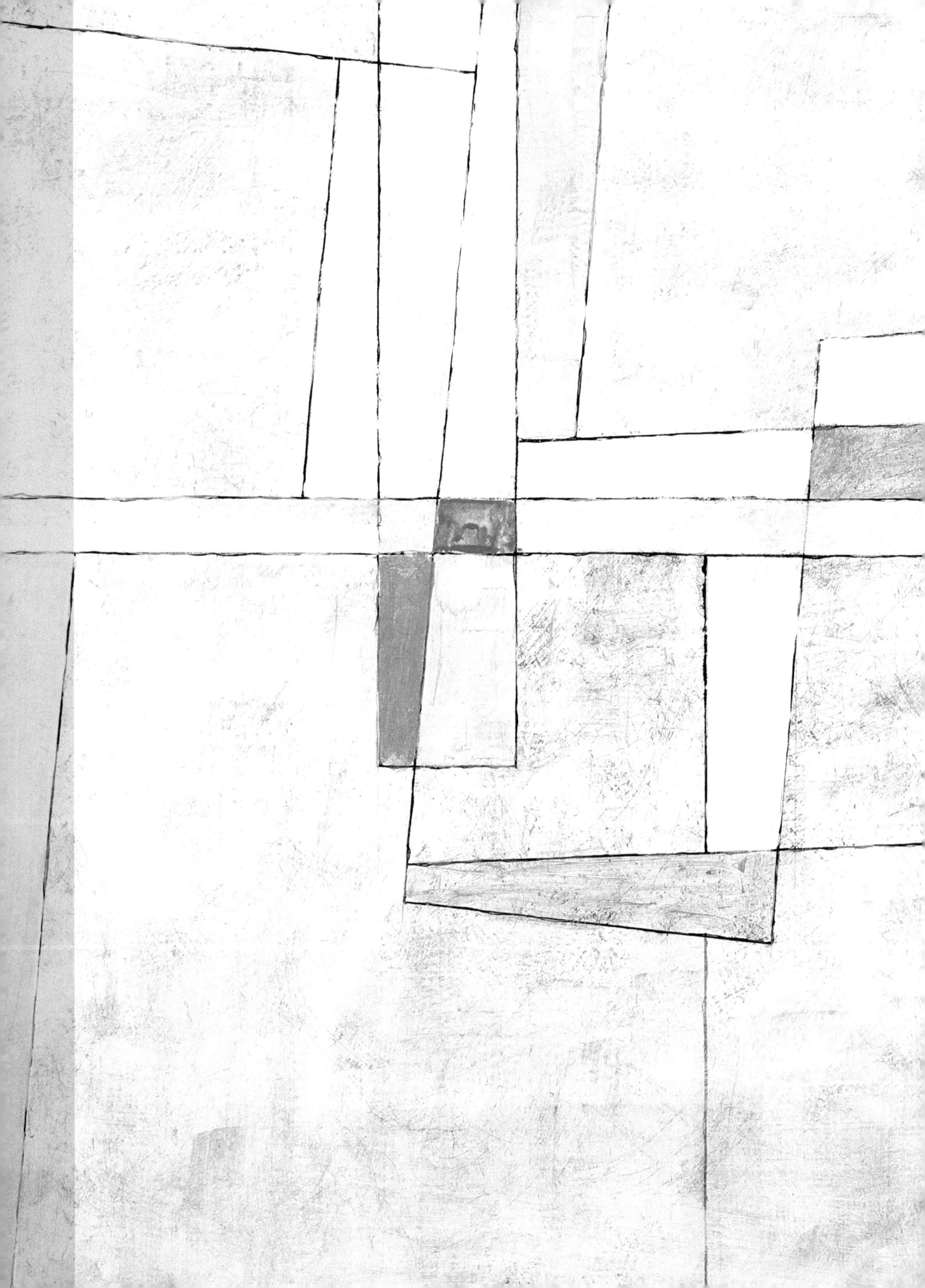

Strategies for Enhancing the Deliberate Practice Exercises

Part III consists of one chapter, Chapter 3, that provides additional advice and instructions for trainers and trainees so that they can reap more benefits from the deliberate practice exercises in Part II. Chapter 3 offers six key points for getting the most out of deliberate practice, advice for monitoring the trainee–trainer, and more specific guidance for trainers and trainees.

How to Get the Most Out of Deliberate Practice: Additional Guidance for Trainers and Trainees

In Chapter 2 and in the exercises themselves, we provide instructions for completing the deliberate practice exercises. This chapter provides guidance on big-picture topics that trainers will need to successfully integrate deliberate practice into their training program. This guidance is based on relevant research and the experiences and feedback from trainers at more than a dozen psychotherapy training programs who volunteered to test the deliberate practice exercises in this book. We cover topics including evaluation, getting the most from deliberate practice, the trainer–trainee relationship, responsive communication, guidance for trainers, and guidance for trainees.

Six Key Points for Getting the Most From Deliberate Practice

Following are six key points of advice for trainers and trainees to get the most benefits from the motivational interviewing (MI) deliberate practice exercises.

Key Point 1: The Setup for the Practice Is Crucial

The exercises in this book are set up to provide an opportunity to practice the micro skills in MI in small, manageable chunks. For full benefit, read the instructions carefully and make sure that all involved have a shared understanding of the purpose of the exercise, the particular skill being practiced, and the process to be practiced. The instructions include a description of how the skill fits in the larger context of MI. For example, all of the exercises include a component of reflective listening practice. There is a reason for this. Learning to listen deeply to the client and to build capacity for receiving, understanding, and reflecting the client's offerings is fundamental to developing MI proficiency. Every exercise is an opportunity to deepen this skill.

Key Point 2: Discover How to Be in the MI Spirit

MI is both a way of being with clients and a way of working with clients. While many of the exercises focus on the technical components of MI (i.e., reflecting ambivalence or evoking

https://doi.org/10.1037/0000297-017

Deliberate Practice in Motivational Interviewing, by J. K. Manuel, D. Ernst, A. Vaz, and T. Rousmaniere

change talk), the deeper practice involves performing the responses while also practicing being grounded in the spirit of MI. Without the collaborative, evocative, accepting, and compassionate mind- and heart-set, the techniques are like a series of notes without the "music." They can be seen as manipulation or trying to trick people into changing. Comfort and proficiency with MI spirit one can improve with practice. Each person will grow into the spirit of MI a bit differently.

Key Point 3: You Can Learn a Lot From Being in the Client Role

MI is a client-centered approach that typically requires an openness in mind and heart to perceive the client's world. The exercises in this book provide an opportunity for the trainee in the client role to practice syncing with the client statement, building empathy for the client, reflecting deeply on the possible meanings of the client statement, and exploring what the client's world might be like. In MI, a single client statement might be considered the tip of the iceberg: Underlying each statement is a vast array of possible meanings, emotions, and connections with personal values and goals. When trainees are role-playing the MI exercises, they should deliver the client statements with appropriate emotional expression and "like they mean it." This might include a sense of gravity or intensity in the voice, a slower, more thoughtful pace, or nonverbal responses that are consistent with the statement. The trainee role-playing the client might say the statement a couple of times to get the feel for the client and provide additional opportunities for the clinician to practice. This is useful for providing feedback on how the clinician response was experienced by the client. This is particularly important when practicing the transcript and mock session exercises (Exercises 13 and 14).

Key Point 4: Hone Your Observation Skills

It is clear from MI training research that trainees (and even lifelong learners) benefit from feedback based on observation of their practice (Schwalbe et al., 2014). MI has a long history of process research using MI-specific tools for structured evaluation of interactions. The tools developed at the University of New Mexico can be found at https://casaa.unm.edu/codinginst.html. These tools are used for observation by trainers, coaches, and trainees themselves. Practicing observation requires a person to attend closely to the interaction at both a specific behavioral level and at a big-picture level. In the MI deliberate practice exercises, instructions are included for observers such as a trainer, a peer, or the trainee in the role of the client. This is an opportunity for trainees to develop and build their own observation skills, to view the interaction from a different perspective, to witness the interaction (even if only a single response) and how it is received, and to learn how to attend to specific skills and offer feedback.

Key Point 5: Customize the Exercises to Fit Your Setting and Context for Training

MI as a communication approach is broadly used across many fields and professions. We have tried to cover a variety of those settings in the exercises. However, you may be working with a specific profession (e.g., probation officers) or in a particular setting (e.g., primary care clinic). The terms used in the exercises (*clinician* and *client*) may not be appropriate for your training. We encourage you to adapt the exercises and terms for your training circumstances. You may work with the trainees individually as they practice. However, you may also have more trainees than you can observe at the same time. If that is the case, we encourage you to use peer observers for exercises that lend themselves to observation. As with most things in MI, there is no one right way to conduct these exercises.

Key Point 6: Extend Your Deliberate Practice Beyond Training

In some ways, the exercises in this book provide one way of practicing the skills. The exercises can be practiced outside of the training, whether on one's own or with others. From the training research on MI, we have learned that a clinician is highly unlikely to maintain or build their MI skills without additional practice beyond the initial training (Schwalbe et al., 2014). This research tells us that MI skill decay is expected if trainees don't have additional training or feedback. We encourage trainees who wish to further their MI skills to have a learning plan that includes deliberate practice of specific MI skills. This might include practice exercises from this book and other resources. The mock sessions provide a great opportunity for practice with integrating all of the MI skills. It might also include setting intentional practice goals for work with real clients. Ideally these practice and real sessions can be recorded for later self-observation or for observation and feedback by a coach or supervisor.

Trainee–Trainer Relationship

In MI, the trainee–trainer relationship is modeled after the client–clinician relationship. The trainee is presumed to have the resources within themselves to develop and grow their practice and to be the expert on their own learning style. The trainer is providing expertise in MI, observational skills, and the capacity to facilitate learning. The relationship is collaborative; individual learning goals are developed together; both the trainees' and trainers' expertise are included in the planning. Trainers create the conditions for learning that are grounded in the client-centered approach and provide feedback and guidance in a MI-consistent manner. The training research indicates that there will be trainees who will not improve in MI skills regardless of the amount of training, coaching, and feedback they have (Moyers et al., 2017). The presence of a solid trainee–trainer relationship can help those individuals recognize that MI is not a good fit for them.

As a caveat about the relationship, this trainee–trainer relationship is not conceptualized as a formal clinical supervision relationship. In the supervisory relationship, the supervisor must be ethically accountable to the client in a way that might require taking some action or possibly directing the supervisee in service of preventing harm to a client. It is important in training to be aware of which role one is in at the time and to be transparent with the trainee about that.

Responsive Communication

By design, MI has significant in-the-moment responsivity built into the method. As a client-centered approach, it comes from a long history of attending in the moment to what the client offers and altering responses to convey understanding and seek shared meaning (Miller & Moyers, 2017). The client is considered to be the expert on their own lives, the primary source of solutions, and the author of their own path forward. The underlying assumption is in line with Carl Rogers (1961): Clients have everything they need, all of the wisdom and strength needed to move toward health. The job of the clinician is to facilitate the process by which the client discovers their path, taps into their reasons to move forward, explores their strengths and values, and finally moves toward their own desired goals. The MI spirit also contains all of the necessary conditions to foster growth that were articulated by Rogers. These include acceptance, genuineness, empathy, positive regard, and nonjudgment. The behavioral expression of these conditions and the facilitation of the growth process require a clinician to be highly responsive to what the client says and does in the conversation, to make guesses about what the underlying meaning might be for the client, and to check those guesses out with the client. Practicing deep reflective listening over time increases the clinician's ability to forgo their own interpretations, let go of their own assumptions, and resist the desire to fix the problem. They allow their response to be influenced by the client's response, and in turn, they influence the client's next response.

The technical component of MI is focused on the client's language about change. The process research on MI is clear that more client language in favor of change (change talk) in conjunction with less client language favoring the status quo (sustain talk) is associated with better client outcomes (Magill et al., 2014). In MI, clinicians are trained to differentiate change talk from sustain talk as well as from neutral language. To actively elicit change talk, clinicians are trained in strategies designed to evoke it. They are then trained to respond in the moment differentially to the type of language, building on and reinforcing change talk while minimizing and softening the sustain talk. There are several appropriate responses to change talk when it appears, and there is evidence that training clinicians to respond to change talk will actually reduce the amount of sustain talk that clients offer (Moyers et al., 2017). MI process research also indicates that clients are likely to give you more of what you focus on. So if a clinician reflects change talk, more client change talk is likely to follow (Moyers et al., 2009). The same is true if the clinician reflects sustain talk or neutral talk. These tasks, focusing on particular types of client language, are well-suited to deliberate practice.

Guidance for Trainers

Modeling the Skills

One of the primary tools that a MI trainer has is modeling, demonstrating the skills during the training. You don't have to be an expert in MI or a professional trainer to model MI skills. You just need to be willing to practice the skills along with the trainees. This is particularly important for reflective listening. Demonstrating your desire to understand the trainee's perspective and struggles through listening can add value to the training opportunity. It can also help you tailor the training to meet the trainees where they are (rather than where the trainer might like them to be).

Observation Is Crucial

Feedback on observed practice promotes significant learning by the trainee. From the MI standpoint, observation of very specific skills is the key to growing good skills. The key point on observation provided some guidance on this. For some of the exercises, the observer role is minimal, just requiring a simple determination (e.g., reflection). Others require more nuanced evaluation (e.g., does this double-sided reflection end with change talk?). Exercises 13 and 14 (the transcript exercise and the mock sessions) provide opportunities for observations of more complex processes and responses. We encourage the trainer to have a structure for observation, particularly for the exercises that have gone beyond a single client response. In addition, we are often trained to attend only to what is not working or what is incorrect. MI is a strengths-based approach. It is important for the observer or trainer to cultivate a practice of attending to what is going well in the trainee's work, what strengths they are demonstrating, and when they are demonstrating MI spirit.

Offer MI-Adherent Feedback

Providing feedback on specific MI skills is essential to trainees' learning. However, we have found that how and when the feedback is delivered is key to how the feedback is received and acted on. The following principles are useful in offering trainee feedback:

- When possible, you should offer feedback collaboratively, starting with the trainee's own assessment of both what went well and what they would like to do differently. This should be more than a perfunctory question and answer, requiring some reflection by the trainee. You will often find that the trainee will identify the same things that you are planning to give feedback on. When the trainees provide their own self-assessment and identify areas of growth, this makes the feedback more powerful.

- Ask permission to share your feedback and perhaps by asking the trainee how they would like to receive feedback (e.g., all at once or starting with positive).

- Start your feedback with what went well or something positive about the trainee's performance.

- Select only one item to suggest improvement on. This requires you to prioritize what you observed and let some things go. You can frame the feedback as something to consider. The best suggestion for improvement will often be the one identified by the trainee, if that is applicable.

- Ask the trainee how they think or feel about the feedback and what their next steps might be. Somewhere in the process, it is important to support the trainees' autonomy ("You are the only who can decide what to do with this feedback" or "If it makes sense to you . . .").

- Acknowledging and affirming the trainees' willingness to be vulnerable and receive feedback goes a long way toward having the feedback be well-received.

Be Clear About Your Role

As mentioned in the discussion of the trainer–trainee relationship, it is important to be clear and transparent about what role you are in with the trainee, particularly when giving feedback. Let them know if it is formal supervision, if it includes a more formal evaluation of their skills (e.g., as a teacher grading a final), or if your role is one of a skill coach or just to offer support. Being upfront with this will help create an environment conducive to learning.

Guidance for Trainees

Owning Your Own Practice

You alone are in charge of your clinical practice. You can choose what you would like to learn, how you would like to be with clients, and how you will manage your own internal world in relation to your work. The challenging work of creating and sustaining the practice you desire is up to you. You also know best how you learn, what kind of feedback and coaching works for you, and what gets in the way of your learning. This knowledge will serve you as you determine your learning goals and pursue skill development. In terms of MI, you will also need to decide whether the approach fits for you, if the way of being with clients is suitable to your own style, and which, if any, of the skills you want to make your own.

Practicing Self-Compassion

Be kind to yourself on this journey. Learning new skills and practicing in new ways is difficult and challenging. It requires you to be vulnerable, to expose yourself as a novice, and to take risks in responding to the exercise. Humility and genuineness are important strengths in work of client-centered communication. These may feel uncomfortable and raise anxiety. This is normal and expected. In the same way that we extend compassion and acceptance to clients, please extend them to yourself. What you are asking of yourself is no less than what you ask of clients. Being gentle with yourself will create an environment that makes it easier to learn.

Learning to Listen in Service of Understanding

There is little listening that actually happens in our world. The act of listening is a great gift that you can give someone. Most of us listen so that we can figure out what to say, to interpret the situation, or to provide a counterargument. In MI, and in client-centered communication more generally, listening is in service of a deeper, shared understanding between the clinician and the client. The practice of this type of listening often involves some unlearning of our typical responses and thought patterns. We may experience a desire to fix the problem, correct the situation, express our opinion, or tell someone what to do. Although these responses may be appropriate sometimes, they interfere with the listening to understand that underlies the MI approach. The shared understanding relies on our ability to facilitate the conversation in a way that the client's meaning, values, goals, and hopes are discovered, evoked, and created. Learning to listen in this way is a lifelong practice.

Growing in Self-Evaluation Skills

MI research indicates that most clinicians are not reliable evaluators of their own practice (Miller et al., 2004). They may overestimate or underestimate their skills. This can be remedied with intentional and structured practice in self-evaluation. In a way, this is another form of deliberate practice. To really grow in more accurate self-evaluation, one must learn to observe their own practice in a more objective way. MI has well-structured tools for doing this, all of which require the recording of sessions for review after the fact. Both simple coding systems (counting reflections and questions) and more complex systems (measuring empathy or cultivating change talk) are available. Transcribing your own session can also provide a lot of useful information about your practice and allows you to get inside of the details and examine the process more closely. Working with a coach or peers can also help you refine your self-evaluation skills. The main point is to engage in the effort and keep it up.

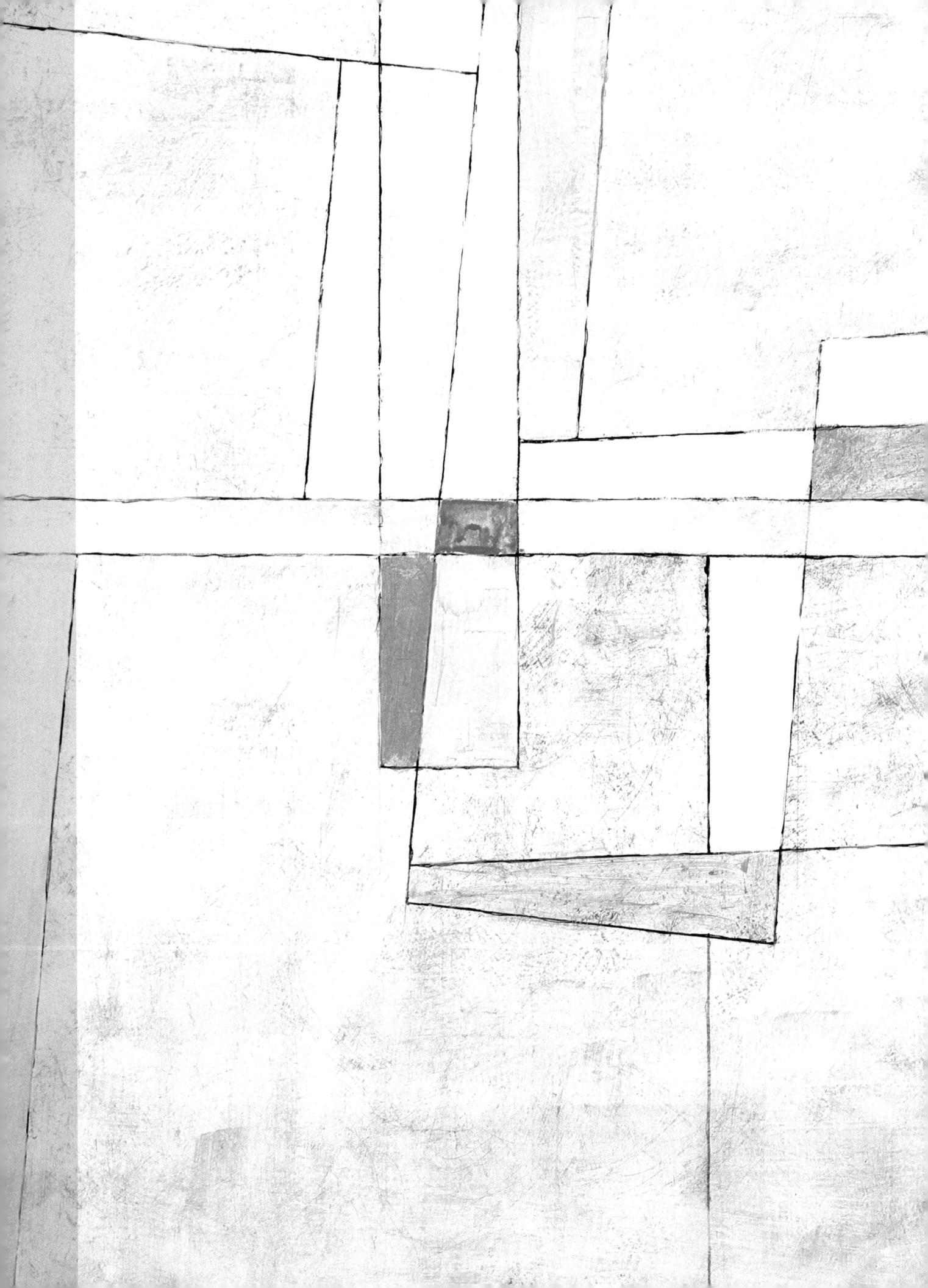

Difficulty Assessments and Adjustments

Deliberate practice works best if the exercises are performed at a good challenge that is neither too hard nor too easy. To ensure that they are practicing at the correct difficulty, trainees should do a *difficulty assessment and adjustment* after each level of client statement is completed (beginner, intermediate, and advanced). To do this, use the following instructions and the Deliberate Practice Reaction Form (Figure A.1), which is also available at https://www.apa.org/pubs/books/deliberate-practice-motivational-interviewing (see the "Clinician and Practitioner Resources" tab). **Do not skip this process!**

How to Assess Difficulty

The *clinician* completes the Deliberate Practice Reaction Form (Figure A.1). If they

- rate the difficulty of the exercise above an 8 or had any of the reactions in the "Too Hard" column, follow the instructions to make the exercise easier;

- rate the difficulty of the exercise below a 4 or didn't have any of the reactions in the "Good Challenge" column, proceed to the next level of harder client statements or follow the instructions to make exercise harder; or

- rate the difficulty of the exercise between 4 and 8 and have at least one reaction in the "Good Challenge" column, do not proceed to the harder client statements but rather repeat the same level.

Making Client Statements Easier

If the clinician ever rates the difficulty of the exercise above an 8 or has any of the reactions in the "Too Hard" column, use the next level easier client statements (e.g., if you were using advanced client statements, switch to intermediate). But if you already were using beginner client statements, use the following methods to make the client statements even easier:

- The person playing the client can use the same beginner client statements but this time in a softer, calmer voice and with a smile. This softens the emotional tone.

FIGURE A.1. Deliberate Practice Reaction Form

Question 1: How challenging was it to fulfill the skill criteria for this exercise?

0   1   2   3   4   5   6   7   8   9   10

← Too Easy →   ← Good →   ← Too Hard →

Question 2: Did you have any reactions in "good challenge" or "too hard" categories? (yes/no)					
Good Challenge			**Too Hard**		
Emotions and Thoughts	Body Reactions	Urges	Emotions and Thoughts	Body Reactions	Urges
Manageable shame, self-judgment, irritation, anger, sadness, etc.	Body tension, sighs, shallow breathing, increased heart rate, warmth, dry mouth	Looking away, withdrawing, changing focus	Severe or overwhelming shame, self-judgment, rage, grief, guilt, etc.	Migraines, dizziness, foggy thinking, diarrhea, disassociation, numbness, blanking out, nausea, etc.	Shutting down, giving up

Too Easy	Good Challenge	Too Hard
⬇	⬇	⬇
Proceed to next difficulty level	Repeat the same difficulty level	Go back to previous difficulty level

Note. From *Deliberate Practice in Emotion-Focused Therapy* (p. 180), by R. N. Goldman, A. Vaz, and T. Rousmaniere, 2021, American Psycho logical Association (https://doi.org/10.1037/0000227–000). Copyright 2021 by the American Psychological Association.

- The client can improvise with topics that are less evocative or make the clinician more comfortable, such as talking about topics without expressing feelings, the future or past (avoiding the here and now), or any topic outside therapy. The clinician can take a short break (5–10 minutes) within the practice.

- The trainer can pause the practice to provide an opportunity for the clinician to think reflectively about the statement. They can use prompts such as "What might be underneath this statement?" "What emotion might the client be experiencing?" or "What might this say about the client's values?" to promote the reflection. They can also help shape the response to meet the criteria of the skill.

Making Client Statements Harder

If the clinician rates the difficulty of the exercise below a 4 or didn't have any of the reactions in the "Good Challenge" column, proceed to next level harder client statements. If you were already using the advanced client statements, the client should make the exercise even harder, using the following guidelines:

- The person playing the client can use the advanced client statements again with a more distressed voice (e.g., very angry, sad, sarcastic) or unpleasant facial expression. This should increase the emotional tone.

- The client can improvise new client statements with topics that are more evocative or make the clinician uncomfortable, such as expressing strong feelings or talking about the here and now, therapy, or the clinician.

- The trainer can pause the practice and encourage the clinician to consider additional responses, focusing on building the guessing muscle, using deeper reflections about underlying meaning, client values, or emotional undertones.

Note. The purpose of a deliberate practice session is not to get through all the client statements and clinician responses but rather to spend as much time as possible practicing at the correct difficulty level. This may mean that trainees repeat the same statements and responses many times, which is okay as long as the difficulty remains in the "good challenge" level.

Deliberate Practice
Diary Form

This book focuses on deliberate practice methods that involve active, live engagement between trainees and a supervisor. Importantly, deliberate practice can extend beyond these focused training sessions. For example, a trainee might read the client stimuli quietly or aloud and practice their responses independently between sessions with a supervisor. In such cases, it is important for the trainee to speak aloud rather than rehearse silently in one's head. Alternatively, two trainees can practice without the supervisor. Although the absence of a supervisor limits one source of feedback, the peer trainee who is playing the client can serve this role, as they can when a supervisor is present. Importantly, these additional deliberate practice opportunities are intended to take place between focused training sessions with a supervisor. The literature on learning motivational interviewing (MI) is clear that ongoing practice, preferably with feedback on specific MI skills, is essential to developing proficiency in the model. To optimize the quality of the deliberate practice when conducted independently or without a supervisor, we have developed a Deliberate Practice Diary Form that can also be downloaded from the "Clinician and Practitioner Resources" tab at https://www.apa.org/pubs/books/deliberate-practice-motivational-interviewing. This form provides a template for the trainee to record their experience of the deliberate practice activity and, ideally, will aid in the consolidation of learning. This form can also be used as part of the evaluation process with the supervisor but is not necessarily intended for that purpose, and trainees are certainly welcome to bring their experience with the independent practice into the next meeting with the supervisor.

Deliberate Practice Diary Form

Use this form to consolidate learnings from the deliberate practice exercises. Please protect your personal boundaries by only sharing information that you are comfortable disclosing.

Name: _____ Date: _____

Exercise: _____

Question 1. What was helpful or worked well this deliberate practice session? In what way?

Question 2. What was unhelpful or didn't go well this deliberate practice session? In what way?

Question 3. What did you learn about yourself, your current skills, and skills you'd like to keep improving? Feel free to share any details, but only those you are comfortable disclosing.

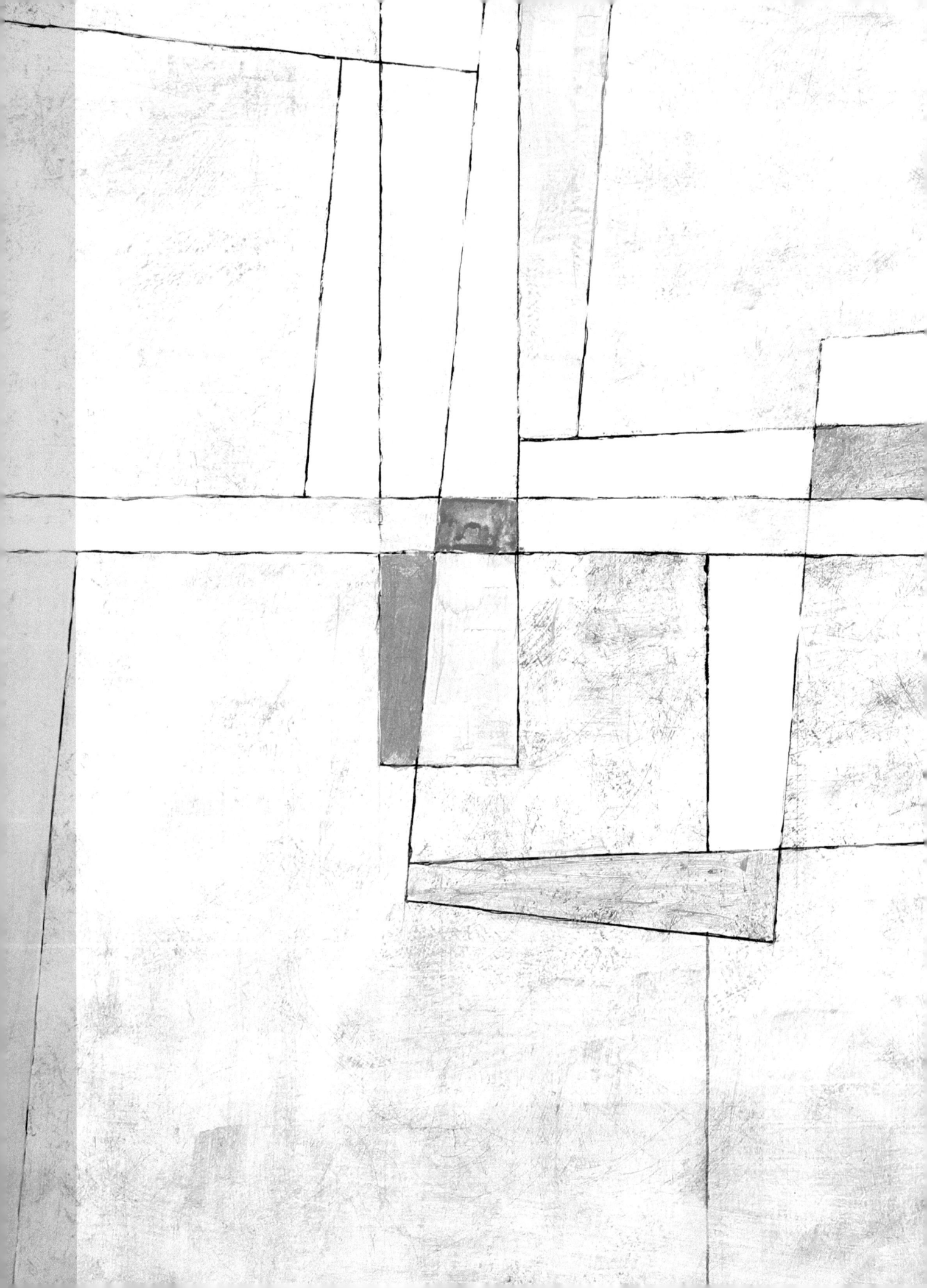

Sample Motivational Interviewing Syllabus With Embedded Deliberate Practice Exercises

This appendix provides a sample one-semester, three-unit course dedicated to teaching motivational interviewing. This course is appropriate for graduate students (master's and doctoral) and medical students at all levels of training, including first-year students who have not yet worked with clients. We present it as a model that can be adopted to a specific program's contexts and needs. For example, instructors may borrow portions of it to use in other courses, in practica, in didactic training events at externships and internships, in workshops, and in continuing education for postgraduate therapists and other health care providers. Additionally, the content may be adapted to fit with different course lengths (e.g., quarter system, all-day courses of shorter duration).

Course Title: Motivational Interviewing: Theory and Deliberate Practice

Course Description

This course teaches theory, principles, and core skills of motivational interviewing (MI). As a course with both didactic and practicum elements, it will review key MI principles and foster the use of deliberate practice to enable students to acquire key MI skills.

Course Objectives

Students who complete this course will be able to

1. Describe the core theory, research, and skills of MI
2. Describe the ways in which MI is an evidenced-based practice
3. Apply the principles of deliberate practice for career-long clinical skill development
4. Demonstrate key MI skills including open-questions, affirmations, and reflections
5. Understand the role of client ambivalence in the change process
6. Differentiate client change and sustain talk
7. Use strategies to elicit and selectively reinforce client change talk
8. Employ MI with clients from diverse cultural backgrounds

Date	Lecture and Discussion	Skills Lab	Reading
Week 1	Introduction to MI theory, history, and research	Lecture on principles of deliberate practice; deliberate practice research	Miller and Rollnick (2013, Chapters 1–4); Miller and Moyers (2017); Miller and Rollnick (2009)
Week 2	MI foundations; simple reflections	Exercise 1: Simple Reflections	Miller and Rollnick (2013, Chapter 5); Miller and Moyers (2015)
Week 3	MI foundations: complex reflections, part 1	Exercise 2: Complex Reflections, Part 1: Guesses at What the Client Means	Miller and Moyers (2021, Chapter 3); Miller (2000)
Week 4	MI foundations: complex reflections, part 2	Exercise 3: Complex Reflections, Part 2: Guesses at Underlying Client Emotions or Values	Moyers and Miller (2013)
Week 5	Open-ended questions	Exercise 4: Reflections and Open-Ended Questions	Miller and Rollnick (2013, Chapters 6 and 7)
Week 6	Client language: change talk	Exercise 5: Eliciting Change Talk	Miller and Rollnick (2013, Chapters 12 and 13); Miller and Moyers (2021, Chapter 9)
Week 7	Responding to change talk	Exercise 6: Reflecting Change Talk	Miller and Rollnick (2013, Chapter 14)
Week 8	Reflecting client ambivalence: double-sided reflections	Exercise 7: Double-Sided Reflections	Miller and Rollnick (2013, Chapters 15–18)
Week 9	Midterm paper due; self-evaluation	Record mock session and transcribe	Self-evaluation: conduct mock session, record and transcribe
Week 10	Dancing with discord	Exercise 8: Dancing With Discord	Miller and Rose (2009)
Week 11	Affirmations	Exercise 9: Simple and Complex Affirmations	Miller and Moyers (2021, Chapters 5 and 6)
Week 12	Supporting client autonomy	Exercise 10: Autonomy Support	Miller and Moyers (2021, Chapters 4 and 8)
Week 13	Agenda mapping	Exercise 11: Agenda Mapping	Miller and Rollnick (2013, Chapters 8–10); Miller and Moyers (2021, Chapter 7)
Week 14	Information exchange; cultural adaptations of MI	Exercise 12: Elicit-Provide-Elicit	Lee et al. (2019); Miller and Rollnick (2013, Chapters 11 and 19–22); Miller and Moyers (2021, Chapter 10); Oh and Lee (2016)
Week 15	Final paper due; final exam; self-evaluation; skill coaching feedback	Exercises 13 and 14: transcript and mock sessions	Miller and Rollnick (2013, Chapters 23–25); Miller and Moyers (2021, Chapters 2 and 11–14); Moyers et al. (2014)

Format of Class

Lecture and Discussion Class: Each week, there will be one lecture and discussion class for 1.5 hours focusing on MI skills and practice.

MI Skills Lab: Each week, there will be one MI Skills Lab for 1.5 hours. Skills Labs are for practicing MI skills using the exercises in this book. The exercises use therapy simulations (role-plays) with the following goals:

1. Build trainees' skill and confidence for using MI skills with real clients
2. Provide a safe space for experimenting with different MI strategies, without fear of making mistakes
3. Provide plenty of opportunity to explore and "try on" different MI strategies

Mock Sessions: Twice in the semester (Weeks 9 and 15), trainees will do a psychotherapy mock session in the MI Skills Lab. In contrast to highly structured and repetitive deliberate practice exercises, a mock MI session is an unstructured and improvised role-played therapy session. Trainees should record the mock session and transcribe it, paying attention to their use of MI skills throughout the session. Mock sessions let trainees

1. Practice using MI skills responsively
2. Experiment with new skills in an unscripted context
3. Build endurance for working with real clients

Homework

Homework will be assigned each week and will include reading, 1 hour of skills practice with an assigned practice partner, and occasional writing assignments. For the skills practice homework, trainees will repeat the exercise they did for that week's MI Skills Lab. Because the instructor will not be there to evaluate performance, trainees should instead complete the Deliberate Practice Reaction Form, as well as the Deliberate Practice Diary Form, for themselves as a self-evaluation.

Writing Assignments

Students are to write two papers: one due at midterm and one due at the last day of class. Two potential topics for the papers are as follows:

- Exploration of the role of ambivalence in behavior change
- A partial transcript of one of the trainees' therapy cases with a real client or role-play, with discussion from an MI perspective

Vulnerability, Privacy, Confidentiality, and Boundaries

This course is aimed at developing MI skills in an experiential framework and as relevant to clinical work. This course is not psychotherapy or a substitute for psychotherapy. Students should interact at a level of self-disclosure that is personally comfortable and helpful to their own learning. Although becoming aware of internal emotional and psychological processes is necessary for a therapist's development, it is not necessary to reveal all that information to the trainer. It is important for students to sense their own level of safety and privacy. Students are not evaluated on the level of material that they choose to reveal in the class.

Multicultural Orientation

This course is taught in a multicultural context, defined as "how the cultural worldviews, values, and beliefs of the client and therapist interact and influence one another to co-create a relational experience that is in the spirit of healing" (Davis et al., 2018, p. 3). Core features of the multicultural orientation include cultural comfort, humility, and responding to cultural opportunities (or previously missed opportunities). Throughout this course, students are encouraged to reflect on their own cultural identity and improve their ability to attune with their clients' cultural identities (Hook et al., 2017). For further guidance on this topic and deliberate practice exercises to improve multicultural skills, see the forthcoming book *Deliberate Practice in Multicultural Counseling* (Harris et al., 2022).

Confidentiality

Due to the nature of the material covered in this course, there are occasions when personal life experience may be relevant for the learning environment. You will not be required to share personal experiences (see the next section), but you might consider doing so when you are comfortable. Additionally, to create a safe learning environment that is respectful of client and therapist information and diversity and to foster open and vulnerable conversation in class, students are required to agree to strict confidentiality within and outside of the instruction setting.

Self-Revealing Information

In accordance with the *Ethical Principles of Psychologists and Code of Conduct* (American Psychological Association, 2017), students are **not required to disclose personal information.** Because this class is about developing both interpersonal and MI competence, following are some important points so that students are fully informed as they make choices to self-disclose:

- Students choose how much, when, and what to disclose. Students are not penalized for the choice not to share personal information.

- The learning environment is susceptible to group dynamics much like any other group space, and therefore students may be asked to share their observations and experiences of the class environment with the singular goal of fostering a more inclusive and productive learning environment.

Evaluation

Self-Evaluation: At the end of the semester (Week 15), trainees will perform a self-evaluation. This will help trainees track their progress and identify areas for further development. The Guidance for Trainees section in Chapter 3 of *Deliberate Practice in Motivational Interviewing* highlights potential areas of focus for self-evaluation.

Grading Criteria

As designed, students would be accountable for the level and quality of their performance in

- the Discussion classes
- the Skills Lab (exercises and mock sessions)
- homework
- midterm and final papers
- a final exam

Required Readings

Lee, C. S., Colby, S. M., Rohsenow, D. J., Martin, R., Rosales, R., McCallum, T. T., Falcon, L., Almeida, J., & Cortés, D. E. (2019). A randomized controlled trial of motivational interviewing tailored for heavy drinking Latinxs. *Journal of Consulting and Clinical Psychology, 87*(9), 815–830. https://doi.org/10.1037/ccp0000428

Miller, W. R. (2000). Rediscovering fire: Small interventions, large effects. *Psychology of Addictive Behaviors, 14*(1), 6–18. https://doi.org/10.1037/0893-164X.14.1.6

Miller, W. R., & Moyers, T. B. (2015). The forest and the trees: Relational and specific factors in addiction treatment. *Addiction, 110*(3), 401–413. https://doi.org/10.1111/add.12693

Miller, W. R., & Moyers, T. B. (2017). Motivational interviewing and the clinical science of Carl Rogers. *Journal of Consulting and Clinical Psychology, 85*(8), 757–766. https://doi.org/10.1037/ccp0000179

Miller, W. R., & Moyers, T. B. (2021). *Effective psychotherapists: Clinical skills that improve client outcomes.* Guilford Press.

Miller, W. R., & Rollnick, S. (2009). Ten things that motivational interviewing is not. *Behavioural and Cognitive Psychotherapy, 37*(2), 129–140. https://doi.org/10.1017/S1352465809005128

Miller, W. R., & Rollnick, S. (2013). *Motivational interviewing: Helping people change* (3rd ed.). Guilford Press.

Miller, W. R., & Rose, G. S. (2009). Toward a theory of motivational interviewing. *American Psychologist, 64*(6), 527–537. https://doi.org/10.1037/a0016830

Moyers, T. B., Manuel, J. K. & Ernst, D. (2014). *Motivational Interviewing Treatment Integrity coding manual 4.1* [Unpublished manual].

Moyers, T. B., & Miller, W. R. (2013). Is low therapist empathy toxic? *Psychology of Addictive Behaviors, 27*(3), 878–884. https://doi.org/10.1037/a0030274

Oh, H., & Lee, C. (2016). Culture and motivational interviewing. *Patient Education and Counseling, 99*(11), 1914–1919. https://doi.org/10.1016/j.pec.2016.06.010

Optional Readings

Arkowitz, H., Miller, W. R., & Rollnick, S. (2017). *Motivational interviewing in the treatment of psychological problems* (2nd ed.). Guilford Press.

Davis, D. E., DeBlaere, C., Owen, J., Hook, J. N., Rivera, D. P., Choe, E., Van Tongeren, D. R., Worthington, E. L., & Placeres, V. (2018). The multicultural orientation framework: A narrative review. *Psychotherapy, 55*(1), 89–100. https://doi.org/10.1037/pst0000160

Hook, J. N., Davis, D. D., Owen, J., & DeBlaere, C. (2017). *Cultural humility: Engaging diverse identities in therapy.* American Psychological Association. https://doi.org/10.1037/0000037-000

Magill, M., Apodaca, T. R., Borsari, B., Gaume, J., Hoadley, A., Gordon, R. E. F., Tonigan, J. S., & Moyers, T. (2018). A meta-analysis of motivational interviewing process: Technical, relational, and conditional process models of change. *Journal of Consulting and Clinical Psychology, 86*(2), 140–157. https://doi.org/10.1037/ccp0000250

Miller, W. R. (2018). *The art of listening well.* Wifp & Stock.

Moyers, T. B., Rowell, L. N., Manuel, J. K., Ernst, D., & Houck, J. M. (2016). The Motivational Interviewing Treatment Integrity code (MITI 4): Rationale, preliminary reliability and validity. *Journal of Substance Abuse Treatment, 65,* 36–42. https://doi.org/10.1016/j.jsat.2016.01.001

Rollnick, S., Miller, W. R., & Butler, C. C. (2007). *Motivational interviewing in health care: Helping patients change behavior.* Guilford Press.

Rosengren, D. B. (2017). *Building motivational interviewing skills: A practitioner workbook* (2nd ed.). Guilford Press.

Wagner, C. C., & Ingersoll, K. S. (2009). Beyond behavior: Eliciting broader change with motivational interviewing. *Journal of Clinical Psychology, 65*(11), 1180–1194. https://doi.org/10.1002/jclp.20639

Wagner, C. C., & Ingersoll, K. S. (2012). *Motivational interviewing in groups.* Guilford Press.

MI With Special Populations: Optional Reading

Hohman, M. (2021). *Motivational interviewing in social work practice.* Guilford Press.

Naar, S., & Suarez, M. (2021). *Motivational interviewing with adolescents and young adults* (2nd ed.). Guilford Press.

Stinson, J. D., & Clark, M. D. (2017). *Motivational interviewing with offenders: Engagement, rehabilitation, and reentry.* Guilford Press.

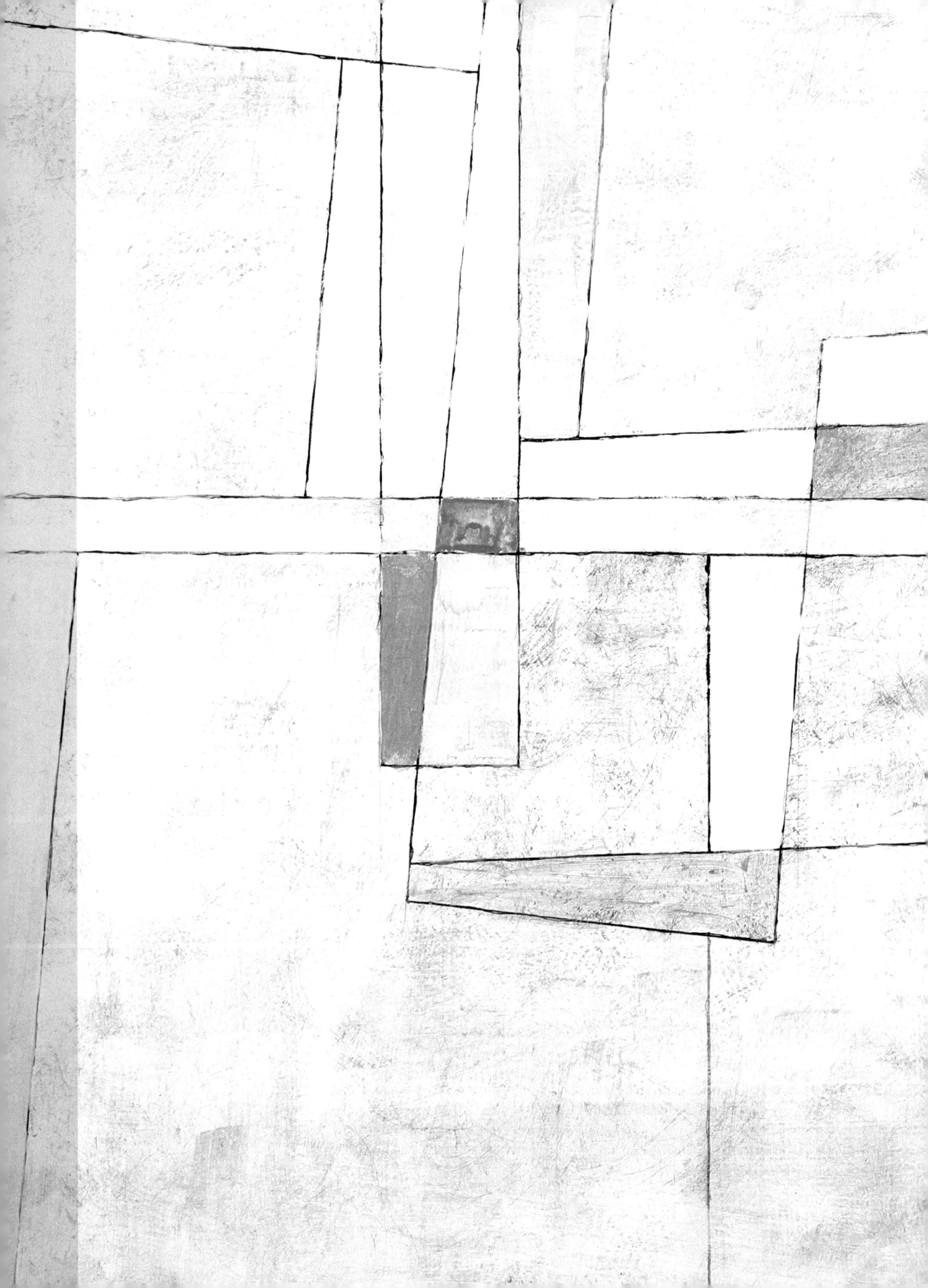

References

American Psychological Association. (2017). *Ethical principles of psychologists and code of conduct* (2002, Amended June 1, 2010, and January 1, 2017). https://www.apa.org/ethics/code/

Anderson, T., Ogles, B. M., Patterson, C. L., Lambert, M. J., & Vermeersch, D. A. (2009). Therapist effects: Facilitative interpersonal skills as a predictor of therapist success. *Journal of Clinical Psychology, 65*(7), 755–768. https://doi.org/10.1002/jclp.20583

Arkowitz, H., Miller, W. R., & Rollnick, S. (2017). *Motivational interviewing in the treatment of psychological problems* (2nd ed.). Guilford Press.

Bailey, R. J., & Ogles, B. M. (2019, August 1). Common factors as a therapeutic approach: What is required? *Practice Innovations, 4*(4), 241–254. https://doi.org/10.1037/pri0000100

Coker, J. (1990). *How to practice jazz.* Jamey Aebersold.

Cook, R. (2005). *It's about that time: Miles Davis on and off record.* Atlantic Books.

Davis, D. E., DeBlaere, C., Owen, J., Hook, J. N., Rivera, D. P., Choe, E., Van Tongeren, D. R., Worthington, E. L., & Placeres, V. (2018). The multicultural orientation framework: A narrative review. *Psychotherapy, 55*(1), 89–100. https://doi.org/10.1037/pst0000160

Decker, S. E., & Martino, S. (2013). Unintended effects of training on clinicians' interest, confidence, and commitment in using motivational interviewing. *Drug and Alcohol Dependence, 132*(3), 681–687. https://doi.org/10.1016/j.drugalcdep.2013.04.022

Ericsson, K. A. (2004). Deliberate practice and the acquisition and maintenance of expert performance in medicine and related domains. *Academic Medicine, 79*(10, Suppl.), S70–S81. https://doi.org/10.1097/00001888-200410001-00022

Ericsson, K. A., Hoffman, R. R., Kozbelt, A., & Williams, A. M. (Eds.). (2018). *The Cambridge handbook of expertise and expert performance* (2nd ed.). Cambridge University Press. https://doi.org/10.1017/9781316480748

Ericsson, K. A., Krampe, R. T., & Tesch-Römer, C. (1993). The role of deliberate practice in the acquisition of expert performance. *Psychological Review, 100*(3), 363–406. https://doi.org/10.1037/0033-295X.100.3.363

Ericsson, K. A., & Pool, R. (2016). *Peak: Secrets from the new science of expertise.* Houghton Mifflin Harcourt.

Fisher, R. P., & Craik, F. I. M. (1977). Interaction between encoding and retrieval operations in cued recall. *Journal of Experimental Psychology: Human Learning and Memory, 3*(6), 701–711. https://doi.org/10.1037/0278-7393.3.6.701

Forman, D. P., & Moyers, T. B. (2019). With odds of a single session, motivational interviewing is a good bet. *Psychotherapy: Theory, Research, & Practice, 56*(1), 62–66. https://doi.org/10.1037/pst0000199

Frey, J., & Hall, A. (2021). *Motivational interviewing for mental health clinicians: A toolkit for skills enhancement.* PESI Publishing.

Gladwell, M. (2008). *Outliers: The story of success.* Little, Brown & Company.

Goldberg, S. B., Rousmaniere, T., Miller, S. D., Whipple, J., Nielsen, S. L., Hoyt, W. T., & Wampold, B. E. (2016). Do psychotherapists improve with time and experience? A longitudinal analysis of outcomes in a clinical setting. *Journal of Counseling Psychology, 63*(1), 1–11. https://doi.org/10.1037/cou0000131

Harris, J., Jin, J., Hoffman, S., Prout, T. A., Rousmaniere, T., & Vaz, A. (2022). *Deliberate practice in multicultural therapy* [Manuscript in preparation].

Hartzler, B., Baer, J. S., Dunn, C., Rosengren, D. B., & Wells, E. (2007). What is seen through the looking glass: The impact of training on practitioner self-rating of motivational interviewing skills. *Behavioural and Cognitive Psychotherapy, 35*(4), 431–445. https://doi.org/10.1017/S1352465807003712

Hatcher, R. L. (2015). Interpersonal competencies: Responsiveness, technique, and training in psychotherapy. *American Psychologist, 70*(8), 747–757. https://doi.org/10.1037/a0039803

Hill, C. E., Kivlighan, D. M., III, Rousmaniere, T., Kivlighan, D. M., Jr., Gerstenblith, J. A., & Hillman, J. W. (2020). Deliberate practice for the skill of immediacy: A multiple case study of doctoral student therapists and clients. *Psychotherapy: Theory, Research, & Practice, 57*(4), 587–597. https://doi.org/10.1037/pst0000247

Hook, J. N., Davis, D. D., Owen, J., & DeBlaere, C. (2017). *Cultural humility: Engaging diverse identities in therapy.* American Psychological Association. https://doi.org/10.1037/0000037-000

Koziol, L. F., & Budding, D. E. (2012). Procedural learning. In N. M. Seel (Ed.), *Encyclopedia of the sciences of learning* (pp. 2694–2696). Springer. https://doi.org/10.1007/978-1-4419-1428-6_670

Lee, C. S., Colby, S. M., Rohsenow, D. J., Martin, R., Rosales, R., McCallum, T. T., Falcon, L., Almeida, J., & Cortés, D. E. (2019). A randomized controlled trial of motivational interviewing tailored for heavy drinking Latinxs. *Journal of Consulting and Clinical Psychology, 87*(9), 815–830. https://doi.org/10.1037/ccp0000428

Lundahl, B., & Burke, B. L. (2009). The effectiveness and applicability of motivational interviewing: A practice-friendly review of four meta-analyses. *Journal of Clinical Psychology, 65*(11), 1232–1245. https://doi.org/10.1002/jclp.20638

Magill, M., Gaume, J., Apodaca, T. R., Walthers, J., Mastroleo, N. R., Borsari, B., & Longabaugh, R. (2014, December). The technical hypothesis of motivational interviewing: A meta-analysis of MI's key causal model. *Journal of Consulting and Clinical Psychology, 82*(6), 973–983. https://doi.org/10.1037/a0036833

McGaghie, W. C., Issenberg, S. B., Barsuk, J. H., & Wayne, D. B. (2014). A critical review of simulation-based mastery learning with translational outcomes. *Medical Education, 48*(4), 375–385. https://doi.org/10.1111/medu.12391

Miller, W. R. (2000). Rediscovering fire: Small interventions, large effects. *Psychology of Addictive Behaviors, 14*(1), 6–18. https://doi.org/10.1037/0893-164X.14.1.6

Miller, W. R., & Moyers, T. B. (2015). The forest and the trees: Relational and specific factors in addiction treatment. *Addiction, 110*(3), 401–413. https://doi.org/10.1111/add.12693

Miller, W. R., & Moyers, T. B. (2017). Motivational interviewing and the clinical science of Carl Rogers. *Journal of Consulting and Clinical Psychology, 85*(8), 757–766. https://doi.org/10.1037/ccp0000179

Miller, W. R., & Moyers, T. B. (2021). *Effective psychotherapists: Clinical skills that improve client outcomes.* Guilford Press.

Miller, W. R., Moyers, T. B., & Rollnick, S. (n.d.). *Motivational interviewing: Helping people change video series.* The Change Companies. https://www.changecompanies.net/products/motivational-interviewing-videos/

Miller, W. R., & Rollnick, S. (1991). *Motivational interviewing: Preparing people to change addictive behavior.* Guilford Press.

Miller, W. R., & Rollnick, S. (2002). *Motivational interviewing: Preparing people for change* (2nd ed.). Guilford Press.

Miller, W. R., & Rollnick, S. (2009). Ten things that motivational interviewing is not. *Behavioural and Cognitive Psychotherapy, 37*(2), 129–140. https://doi.org/10.1017/S1352465809005128

Miller, W. R., & Rollnick, S. (2013). *Motivational interviewing: Helping people change* (3rd ed.). Guilford Press.

Miller, W. R., & Rose, G. S. (2009). Toward a theory of motivational interviewing. *American Psychologist, 64*(6), 527–537. https://doi.org/10.1037/a0016830

Miller, W. R., Yahne, C. E., Moyers, T. B., Martinez, J., & Pirritano, M. (2004). A randomized trial of methods to help clinicians learn motivational interviewing. *Journal of Consulting and Clinical Psychology, 72*(6), 1050–1062. https://doi.org/10.1037/0022-006X.72.6.1050

Moyers, T. B., Houck, J., Glynn, L. H., Hallgren, K. A., & Manuel, J. K. (2017, March 1). A randomized controlled trial to influence client language in substance use disorder treatment. *Drug and Alcohol Dependence, 172*, 43–50. https://doi.org/10.1016/j.drugalcdep.2016.11.036

Moyers, T. B., Manuel, J. K., & Ernst, D. (2014). *Motivational Interviewing Treatment Integrity coding manual 4.1* [Unpublished manual].

Moyers, T. B., Martin, T., Houck, J. M., Christopher, P. J., & Tonigan, J. S. (2009). From in-session behaviors to drinking outcomes: A causal chain for motivational interviewing. *Journal of Consulting and Clinical Psychology, 77*(6), 1113–1124. https://doi.org/10.1037/a0017189

Moyers, T. B., & Miller, W. R. (2013). Is low therapist empathy toxic? *Psychology of Addictive Behaviors, 27*(3), 878–884. https://doi.org/10.1037/a0030274

Naar, S., & Suarez, M. (2021). *Motivational interviewing with adolescents and young adults* (2nd ed.). Guilford Press.

Norcross, J. C., Lambert, M. J., & Wampold, B. E. (2019). *Psychotherapy relationships that work* (3rd ed.). Oxford University Press.

Oh, H., & Lee, C. (2016). Culture and motivational interviewing. *Patient Education and Counseling, 99*(11), 1914–1919. https://doi.org/10.1016/j.pec.2016.06.010

Pollak, K. I., Nagy, P., Bigger, J., Bilheimer, A., Lyna, P., Gao, X., Lancaster, M., Watkins, R. C., Johnson, F., Batish, S., Skelton, J. A., & Armstrong, S. (2016). Effect of teaching motivational interviewing via communication coaching on clinician and patient satisfaction in primary care and pediatric obesity-focused offices. *Patient Education and Counseling, 99*(2), 300–303. https://doi.org/10.1016/j.pec.2015.08.013

Randall, C. L., & McNeil, D. W. (2017). Motivational interviewing as an adjunct to cognitive behavior therapy for anxiety disorders: A critical review of the literature. *Cognitive and Behavioral Practice, 24*(3), 296–311. https://doi.org/10.1016/j.cbpra.2016.05.003

Rogers, C. (1961). *On becoming a person.* Constable.

Rollnick, S., Miller, W. R., & Butler, C. C. (2007). *Motivational interviewing in health care: Helping patients change behavior.* Guilford Press.

Rosengren, D. B. (2017). *Building motivational interviewing skills: A practitioner workbook* (2nd ed.). Guilford Press.

Rousmaniere, T. G. (2016). *Deliberate practice for psychotherapists: A guide to improving clinical effectiveness.* Routledge. https://doi.org/10.4324/9781315472256

Rousmaniere, T. (2019). *Mastering the inner skills of psychotherapy: A deliberate practice manual.* Gold Lantern Books.

Rousmaniere, T. G., Goodyear, R., Miller, S. D., & Wampold, B. E. (Eds.). (2017). *The cycle of excellence: Using deliberate practice to improve supervision and training.* Wiley-Blackwell. https://doi.org/10.1002/9781119165590

Rubak, S., Sandbaek, A., Lauritzen, T., & Christensen, B. (2005). Motivational interviewing: A systematic review and meta-analysis. *The British Journal of General Practice, 55*(513), 305–312.

Sayegh, C. S., Huey, S. J., Zara, E. J., & Jhaveri, K. (2017). Follow-up treatment effects of contingency management and motivational interviewing on substance use: A meta-analysis. *Psychology of Addictive Behaviors, 31*(4), 403–414. https://doi.org/10.1037/adb0000277

Schwalbe, C. S., Oh, H. Y., & Zweben, A. (2014). Sustaining motivational interviewing: A meta-analysis of training studies. *Addiction, 109*(8), 1287–1294. https://doi.org/10.1111/add.12558

Smith, S. M. (1979). Remembering in and out of context. *Journal of Experimental Psychology: Human Learning and Memory, 5*(5), 460–471. https://doi.org/10.1037/0278-7393.5.5.460

Squire, L. R. (2004). Memory systems of the brain: A brief history and current perspective. *Neurobiology of Learning and Memory, 82*(3), 171–177. https://doi.org/10.1016/j.nlm.2004.06.005

Steinberg, M. P., & Miller, W. R. (2015). *Motivational interviewing in diabetes care.* Guilford Press.

Stiles, W. B., Honos-Webb, L., & Surko, M. (1998). Responsiveness in psychotherapy. *Clinical Psychology: Science and Practice, 5*(4), 439–458. https://doi.org/10.1111/j.1468-2850.1998.tb00166.x

Stiles, W. B., & Horvath, A. O. (2017). Appropriate responsiveness as a contribution to therapist effects. In L. G. Castonguay & C. E. Hill (Eds.), *How and why are some therapists better than others? Understanding therapist effects* (pp. 71–84). American Psychological Association. https://doi.org/10.1037/0000034-005

Stinson, J. D., & Clark, M. D. (2017). *Motivational interviewing with offenders: Engagement, rehabilitation, and reentry.* Guilford Press.

Taylor, J. M., & Neimeyer, G. J. (2017). The ongoing evolution of continuing education: Past, present, and future. In T. G. Rousmaniere, R. Goodyear, S. D. Miller, & B. Wampold (Eds.), *The cycle of excellence: Using deliberate practice to improve supervision and training* (pp. 219–248). John Wiley & Sons. https://doi.org/10.1002/9781119165590.ch11

Tracey, T. J. G., Wampold, B. E., Goodyear, R. K., & Lichtenberg, J. W. (2015). Improving expertise in psychotherapy. *Psychotherapy Bulletin, 50*(1), 7–13.

Wagner, C. C., & Ingersoll, K. S. (2012). *Motivational interviewing in groups.* Guilford Press.

Index

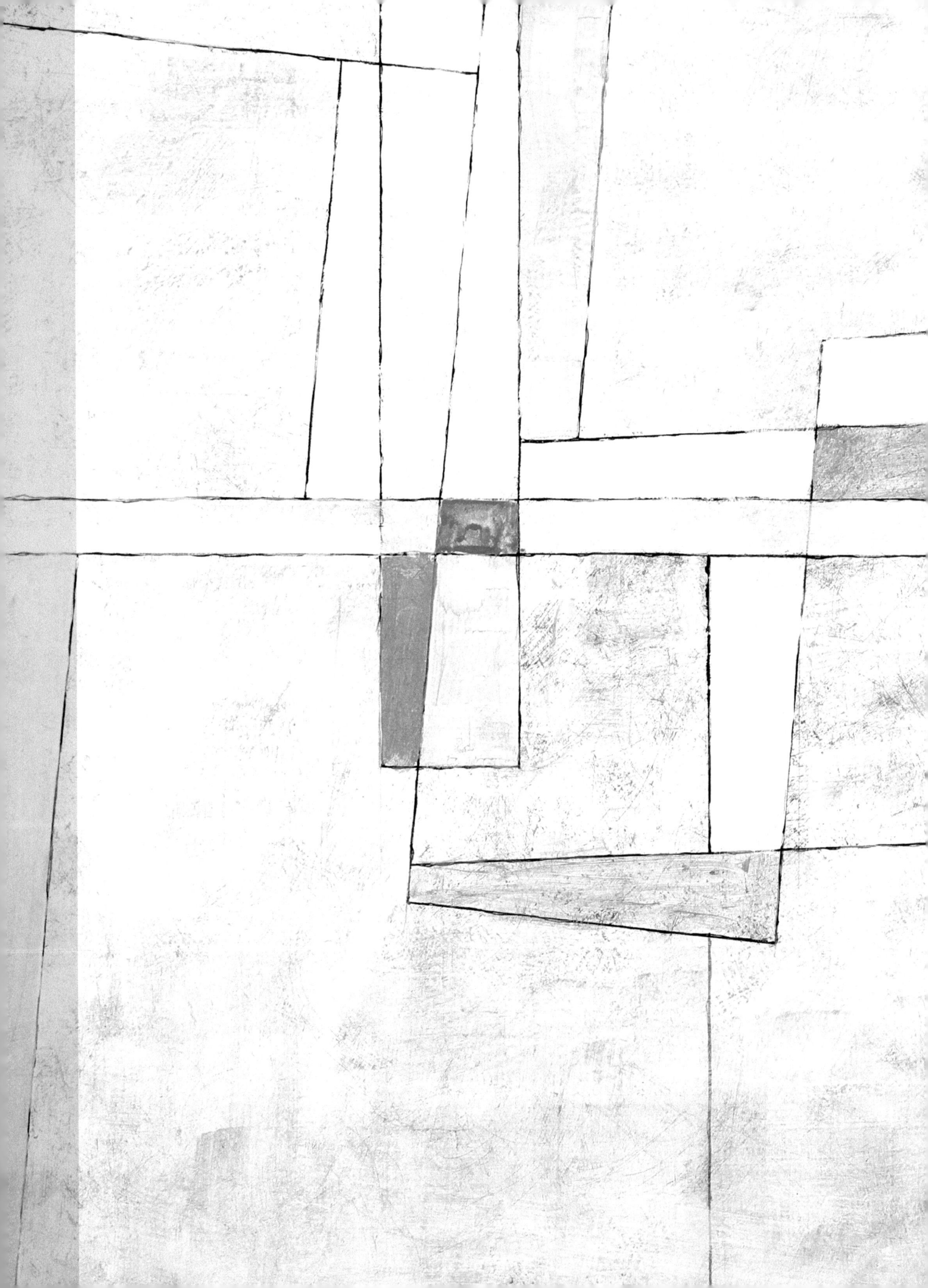

About the Authors

Jennifer K. Manuel, PhD, is the deputy director of psychology at the San Francisco Veterans Affairs Health Care System and an associate professor in the Department of Psychiatry and Behavioral Sciences at the University of California, San Francisco. She has been a member of the Motivational Interviewing Network of Trainers, an international organization committed to promoting high-quality motivational interviewing (MI) practice and training, since 2005. She conducts MI training and MI coding training workshops throughout the United States and internationally. She has coauthored multiple MI behavioral coding systems including the widely used Motivational Interviewing Treatment Integrity coding manual. Dr. Manuel's research expertise is in the implementation and evaluation of MI in front-line clinical settings. She has served as an investigator on several trials examining the effectiveness of MI and on MI training methods.

Denise Ernst, PhD, is an adjunct professor at the School of Social Work, Portland State University, Portland, Oregon. She has been a motivational interviewing (MI) consultant for more than 25 years, providing training, evaluation, research support, implementation support, and private coaching. Dr. Ernst has participated in the development and refinement of the family of MI coding instruments, including the Motivational Interviewing Skill Code and the Motivational Interviewing Treatment Integrity coding system, used to determine treatment fidelity, practitioner skills, and the critical elements of good MI practice. She participated in research efforts to enhance training effects, providing structured feedback and coaching for individuals from many different professions who were learning MI. Dr. Ernst has been a member of the Motivational Interviewing Network of Trainers since 1997 and has overseen the evaluation of applicant work samples as part of the admission process for the past 10 years. This has included extensive training and consultation internationally.

Alexandre Vaz, PhD, is cofounder and chief academic officer of Sentio University, Los Angeles, California. He provides deliberate practice workshops and advanced clinical training and supervision to clinicians around the world. Dr. Vaz is the author and coeditor of four books on deliberate practice and psychotherapy training and two series of clinical training books: The Essentials of Deliberate Practice (American Psychological Association) and Advanced Therapeutics, Clinical and Interpersonal Skills (Elsevier). He has held multiple committee roles for the Society for the Exploration of Psychotherapy Integration and the Society for Psychotherapy Research. Dr. Vaz is founder and host of *Psychotherapy Expert Talks*, an acclaimed interview series with distinguished psychotherapists and therapy researchers.

Tony Rousmaniere, PsyD, is cofounder and program director of Sentio University, Los Angeles, California. He provides workshops, webinars, and advanced clinical training and supervision to clinicians around the world. Dr. Rousmaniere is the author and coeditor of six books on deliberate practice and psychotherapy training and two series of clinical training books: The Essentials of Deliberate Practice (American Psychological Association) and Advanced Therapeutics, Clinical and Interpersonal Skills (Elsevier). In 2017, he published a widely cited article in *The Atlantic Monthly*, "What Your Therapist Doesn't Know." Dr. Rousmaniere supports the open-data movement and publishes his aggregated clinical outcome data, in deidentified form, on his website at https://www.drtonyr.com/. A Fellow of the American Psychological Association, Dr. Rousmaniere was awarded the Early Career Award by the Society for the Advancement of Psychotherapy (APA Division 29).